Shipwrecks and the
Maritime History of Singapore

Shipwrecks and the
Maritime History of Singapore

edited by **Kwa Chong Guan**

 YUSOF ISHAK
INSTITUTE

First published in Singapore in 2023 by
ISEAS Publishing
30 Heng Mui Keng Terrace
Singapore 119614

Email: publish@iseas.edu.sg
Website: bookshop.iseas.edu.sg

The responsibility for facts and opinions in this publication rests exclusively with the authors and their interpretations do not necessarily reflect the views or the policy of the publisher or its supporters.

ISEAS Library Cataloguing-in-Publication Data

Name(s): Kwa, Chong Guan, editor.
Title: Shipwrecks and the maritime history of Singapore / Kwa Chong Guan, editor.
Description: Singapore : ISEAS-Yusof Ishak Institute, 2023. | Includes index.
Identifiers: ISBN 9789815104271 (hardcover) | ISBN 9789815104479 (PDF) | ISBN 9789815104486 (epub)
Subjects: LCSH: Shipwrecks—Singapore. | Navigation—History—Singapore. | Underwater archaeology—Singapore. | Entrepôt trade—Singapore—History.
Classification: LCC VK1288 S6S55

Cover design by Lee Meng Hui
Copyediting and typesetting by Stephen Logan
Printed in Singapore by Markono Print Media Pte Ltd

Contents

Foreword

On 18 May 2015, marine salvage master Mr Ramdzan Salim informed our Archaeology Unit (AU) about a possible historic shipwreck he had found during salvage work on a capsized barge in the vicinity of Pedra Branca. In his email were photographs of coral-encrusted green plates that he had recovered from the seabed. Dr Michael Flecker and the staff of the AU had no difficulty identifying the coral-encrusted plates as fourteenth-century celadon plates from the Longquan kilns in Zhejiang Province, China. Our AU colleagues met Mr Salim and one of his divers on 22 May to confirm the finds and its location.

A year-long process of discussions and planning with the National Heritage Board (NHB) followed before an exploratory survey was launched to confirm that the recovered Chinese celadons were part of the cargo of a ship that had sunk in the vicinity of Pedra Branca. Thereafter the NHB commissioned the AU to undertake the excavation of the wreck over the next three years.

Dr Flecker's essay in this volume summarizes the results of this three-year archaeological excavation of the shipwreck, which recovered some four tonnes of Chinese ceramics. A follow-up survey of the vicinity located another shipwreck, which was excavated from 2019 to 2021 and has been identified as an eighteenth-century country trader.

The essays in this book by Temasek History Research Centre (THRC) alumni are the first to provide a historical context of these two shipwrecks since the public announcement of their discovery on 16 June 2021. These essays developed from presentations at a THRC webinar on these two shipwrecks in early April 2022. I would like to thank my colleagues for accepting our invitation to share their preliminary ideas on these two wrecks with a wider audience.

The excavation of these two historic shipwrecks was the most complex and longest archaeological investigation undertaken by the AU since its establishment in 2010. To be sure, archaeological excavations in Singapore began relatively late, in 1984 on Fort Canning. Thus far, the AU has undertaken excavations at Fort Canning Hill, Empress Place, Adam Park, the National Gallery Singapore and the Victoria Memorial Hall.

The AU has also participated in field schools with archaeological institutions in Cambodia and Indonesia. These field schools have brought together young scholars and archaeologists from Southeast Asia to network, cooperate and learn from each other in investigating archaeological sites in Phnom Kulen at Angkor, Banten Lama in West Java and Trawas in East Java.

The discovery of not one but two historic shipwrecks opens a new chapter in Singapore's archaeology, one that takes it beyond Fort Canning and its environs into the seas around Singapore. These two shipwrecks, as the essays in this volume outline, open new vistas for our understanding of Singapore's pre-modern and modern history. But much more research needs to be done to augment the arguments developed in these essays, which are based on the preliminary reports of the excavation of these two wrecks by Dr Flecker. The bulk of the artefacts recovered from these two wrecks are currently being cleaned and sorted, and they await analysis. The AU is committed to documenting these two wrecks and making the findings available for others to consult.

On behalf of the AU, I would like to thank NHB for supporting and underwriting the excavation of the two wrecks and other government agencies for their support and advice.

I am grateful to Mr Ramdzan Salim and his colleagues, who were sufficiently sharp-eyed to notice the stacks of coral-encrusted plates around the capsized barge they were salvaging as possibly significant historical artefacts and bring them to our attention. Their civic-mindedness has allowed us to conduct these maritime excavations and open up new understanding and framings of Singapore's past.

Finally, my thanks also to Adjunct Associate Professor Kwa Chong Guan, our Associate Fellow, whose energy and drive have made the webinars and this book possible. Adjunct Associate Professor Kwa's intellectual leadership has been vital to this project. I am also grateful to our Research Officers Benjamin Khoo and Fong Sok Eng for their stellar work behind the scenes.

Terence Chong
Head, Archaeology Unit
Director, Research, and Deputy Chief Executive, ISEAS

Acknowledgements

The essays in this book are revisions of presentations delivered at a Temasek History Research Centre webinar in early April 2022. The authors and editor thank Dr Terence Chong, Deputy Chief Executive of ISEAS, for his support for the convening of this webinar during its long nine-month gestation and eventual publication of this book. We also thank Mr Stephen Logan at ISEAS Publishing for copyediting and typesetting this book, and Mr Benjamin Khoo and Ms Fong Sok Eng for yeomen service in coordinating the successive drafts and revisions of these essays and sourcing of illustrations in the book.

Contributors

Kwa Chong Guan

Kwa Chong Guan is an Associate Fellow at the Temasek History Research Centre and Adjunct (Hon.) Associate Professor at the History Department, National University of Singapore. He is a co-author with Derek Heng, Peter Borschberg and Tan Tai Yong of *Seven Hundred Years: A History of Singapore* (Singapore: National Library Board, 2019). Kwa chairs the National Heritage Board's Archaeology Advisory Panel and is a Senior Fellow at the S. Rajaratnam School of International Studies, Nanyang Technological University, where he works on a range of emerging regional security issues.

Peter Borschberg

Peter Borschberg teaches history at NUS. He has authored several studies on pre-1800 Singapore and the Straits region, including *The Singapore and Melaka Straits: Violence, Security and Diplomacy in the 17th Century* (2010), *Singapore in the Cycles of the Longue Durée* (JMBRAS, 2017) and *The Port of Singapore c.1290–1819: Evidence, Frameworks and Challenges* (JMBRAS, 2018).

Michael Flecker

Michael Flecker, Managing Director of Maritime Explorations, has overseen some of the most important shipwreck excavations in Asia over the past thirty years. They include the ninth-century Belitung (Tang), twelfth-century Flying Fish, thirteenth-century Java Sea, fifteenth-century Bakau, *c.*1608 Binh Thuan and *c.*1690 Vung Tau wrecks. He earned his PhD from the National University of Singapore based on the excavation of the tenth-century Intan Wreck, and he specializes in ancient Asian ship construction and maritime trade. He has twice been a Visiting Fellow at the Nalanda-Sriwijaya Centre and is presently a Senior Visiting Fellow at the Archaeology Unit, ISEAS – Yusof Ishak Institute.

Derek Heng

Derek Heng is currently Professor and Department Chair at the Department of History, Northern Arizona University. He was Associate Professor of Humanities and Head of Studies (History) at Yale-NUS College and was previously Head of NSC from January 2014 to July 2015. He specializes in the trans-regional history of Maritime Southeast Asia and the South China Sea during the first and early second millennia AD, and is the author of *Sino-Malay Trade and Diplomacy in the Tenth through the Fourteenth Century* (Athens: Ohio University Press, 2009) and co-author of *Seven Hundred Years: A History of Singapore* (Singapore: National Library Board, 2019). He has also authored a number of journal articles and book chapters on the Chinese material remains recovered from archaeological sites in Southeast Asia, as well as having edited three volumes on the history and historiography of Singapore's past. He is currently working on methods in integrating archaeological data from Southeast Asia with Chinese digital textual databases. He maintains a keen interest on the historiography of Singapore, and he has edited *New Perspectives and Sources on the History of Singapore: A Multi-Disciplinary Approach* (Singapore: National Library Board, 2006), *Reframing Singapore: Memory, Identity and Trans-Regionalism,* ICAS Series volume 6 (Amsterdam: Amsterdam University Press, 2009) and *Singapore in Global History* (Amsterdam: Amsterdam University Press, 2011).

Benjamin J.Q. Khoo

Benjamin J.Q. Khoo is currently a Research Associate at the Asia Research Institute, National University of Singapore. He was previously a Research Officer at the Temasek History Research Centre at the ISEAS – Yusof Ishak Institute and also formerly a Lee Kong Chian Research Fellow at the National Library of Singapore. He has recently authored articles with Peter Borschberg on the circulation of knowledge of pre-1800 Singapore and the Straits region. His research is focused on early modern cultural and diplomatic encounters in Asia.

1

Introduction: Two Historical Shipwrecks and Their Implications for Singapore History

Kwa Chong Guan

The National Heritage Board (NHB) and the ISEAS – Yusof Ishak Institute announced on 16 June 2021 the successful archaeological excavation of two historic shipwrecks in the eastern approaches to Singapore's waters. The first shipwreck was discovered in 2015 in the course of salvage work on a barge that had run aground on a prominent rock outcrop known for more than a millennium as a major hazard to mariners approaching the Strait of Singapore. The National Heritage Board commissioned the Archaeology Unit of the ISEAS – Yusof Ishak Institute to investigate and then excavate the wreck in 2016. This wreck, intermittently excavated for the next three years, has now been identified from its cargo of Chinese ceramics to be a fourteenth-century vessel most likely headed for Temasek, and therefore named the Temasek Wreck.

A survey and search of the vicinity for other wrecks, commissioned in mid-2019, found a second wreck, which was excavated over the next two years. The second shipwreck has been identified from archival research as an eighteenth-century merchant ship, the *Shah Muncher,* which was commissioned and owned by the Bombay trader and ship owner Sorabjee Muncherjee Readymoney. It was built in India in 1789 and sank on its return voyage from China to India in 1796 with a diverse cargo of Chinese ceramics and other non-ceramic trade items ranging from glass to copper-alloy objects and umbrellas. There would have been other trade commodities, especially tea, which would have perished. At a thousand tonnes the *Shah Muncher* was similar in size to the larger East India Company (EIC) ships sailing between England and China.

The essays in this book provide the context of these two wrecks and their implications for our understanding of Singapore history. The two lead essays describing the wrecks and locating them in the context of other contemporary shipwrecks are by Michael Flecker, who brought thirty years of experience and expertise as a marine archaeologist to the excavation of these two shipwrecks. His essays here are summaries of more detailed preliminary reports published by the ISEAS – Yusof Ishak Institute.[1]

Questions about Singapore History

The recovery of these two wrecks raises a number of questions about our understanding of Singapore history that we should have, but have not, asked. For the Temasek Wreck, were the 4.4 tonnes of ceramics recovered all destined for fourteenth-century Temasek? If so, then it raises further questions regarding the size and nature of Temasek's market to absorb that volume of ceramics, which included some of the newest blue-and-white ceramics being produced in the kilns of Jingdezhen. These questions are discussed by Derek Heng in his essay in this volume. The *Shah Muncher* Wreck raises other issues of who were the merchants owning and operating other similar ships trading between China and India? Using the *Shah Muncher* as an example, Peter Borschberg discusses the EIC's system of trade between Britain and India, which it had a royal monopoly of, and its intra-Asian trade. The Company rationalized this parallel trade as the *country trade*. And it was these country traders who were to become central to Singapore's historical development in the first half of the nineteenth century.

These two historic shipwrecks challenge us to view Singapore from the sea, from the deck of the *Shah Muncher*, or the fourteenth-century ship headed for Temasek with its cargo of ceramics, rather than from Fort Canning, the seat of government in the fourteenth century and again in the nineteenth century, and from where the history of Singapore has conventionally been viewed as a colony of the British Empire. What attracted traders and shippers to fourteenth-century Temasek and the EIC station Stamford Raffles established on Singapore? Were there traders and shippers calling at Temasek before the fourteenth century and in the five centuries between Temasek and Singapore in the nineteenth century?

Dr John Crawfurd, the second Resident of Singapore from 1823 to 1826, recorded that,

> For a period of about five centuries and a half, there is no record of Singapore having been occupied, and it was only the occasional resort of pirates. In that year it was taken possession of by the party from whom we [the British] received it, an officer of the government of Jehore called the Tumângung. This person told me himself that he came there with about 150 followers, a few months before the British expedition which afterwards captured Java passed this island, and this happened in the summer of 1811.[2]

Crawfurd was aware of a fourteenth-century settlement on Singapore, of which he saw and recorded the remains of, but was unimpressed by.

The history of Singapore since Crawfurd has been viewed from Government House. It is about the administration and governance of multi-ethnic trading communities that developed behind the quays of the Singapore River, around the Kallang River estuary and, later, the New Harbour at Tanjong Pagar. The sea in front of the port city was not a major concern of colonial governance. The 2 August 1824 treaty that Dr John Crawfurd concluded with Sultan Hussein and the Temenggong was for the ceding of the island of Singapore and "the adjacent seas, straits and islets, to the extent of 10 geographical miles, from the coast of the said main Island of Singapore". This was within the traditional territorial sea limit of four to ten miles claimed by coastal states. The sea beyond this ten-mile limit from Singapore was the high sea, open and free for all to travel across. Singapore's attractiveness to traders then and now depends upon the security of its porous maritime boundaries against piracy, smuggling and other criminal activities.[3] Ensuring the security and safety of the sea beyond the ten-mile limit was assigned to the Royal Navy, the dominant naval power in the region (and also globally).[4]

The fortunes of Singapore and other port cities were subject to systemic geopolitical shifts and competition to control the high seas and its trade by major powers of the day. As the explorer and courtier Sir Walter Raleigh declared in the early seventeenth century, "whoever commands the sea, commands the trade; whosoever commands the trade of the world commands the riches of the world, and consequently the world itself". From this perspective of the imperative to control the sea, "Raffles' acquisition of Singapore", then Raffles Professor of History Wong Lin Ken argued, "was the unforeseen long-term result of Anglo-French rivalry in the Indian subcontinent, the consequent rise of the British Raj, and the need to defend its interests in the Bay of Bengal and the transoceanic route to the Archipelago and China."[5] Two centuries earlier, the Portuguese and the Dutch thought of establishing forts on

Singapore to control the surrounding waterways.[6] Post-1945 Singapore continued to depend upon the Royal Navy, from its old naval base at Sembawang, to ensure the freedom of the high seas for its survival.

Writing Singapore's History from the Sea

Cyril Northcote Parkinson, the inaugural Raffles Professor of History at the then new University of Malaya in 1950, was well placed to pioneer a more maritime framing of Singapore's past. He had published a much-acclaimed work entitled *Trade in the Eastern Seas, 1793–1813* in 1937, which describes vividly how the EIC operated, the goods it traded in, the ships the Company owned and the working conditions of its sailors on these ships.[7] In 1954, Parkinson published a companion study, *War in the Eastern Seas, 1793–1815,* which focussed on the naval campaigns of the Napoleonic wars in the Eastern Seas.[8] However, the priorities of Parkinson and his colleagues were not on exploring the maritime history of the region, but on training their students to reconstruct the histories of Malaya and Singapore, largely on the basis of the 170 volumes of handwritten Straits Settlement Records archived in the old Raffles Museum and Library. It was about writing a local history grounded on colonial foundations, which, after 1965, was transformed into writing a national history of Singapore.

The Singapore Story is about the anti-colonial nationalist struggle for the future of the island.[9] The sea around the island was not an issue. The issues of pirates, smugglers and traders illegally moving commodities— from guns to pepper, opium and tin—and migrations across the seas had largely been brought under control. The challenges confronting the post-1965 city-state included the communalism of its plural society, lacking what then prime minister Lee Kuan Yew described as the "social glue" to hold it together as a modern nation-state, and the threat of communism within the larger geopolitical framework of the Cold War. The freedom of the seas upon which Singapore's survival as a regional entrepôt and city state depended continued to be provided largely by the Royal Navy, from its restored naval base,[10] at least until 1972, and by the US Seventh Fleet.

The sea has thus been taken for granted in the historical development of Singapore, which is perceived to be driven more by Singapore's strategic location—something that Raffles is credited with recognizing. If we subscribe to the claim by Raffles that the British station he established on Singapore "command[s] the Southern entrance of the Straits of Malacca, and combine[s] extraordinary local advantages with a peculiarly admirable Geographical position", then we have the question raised by Wong Lin Ken: "how do we account for Singapore's emergence as a strategic centre of trade linking the sea routes of the South China Sea with the Bay of Bengal and wider Indian Ocean beginning only in the nineteenth century, but not before?"[11] An answer to Wong's quandary lies in an underappreciated 1955 monograph[12] by Dr Carl Alexander Gibson-Hill, the last British director of the old Raffles Museum, on the history of the Old Straits of Singapore.

Viewed from the sea, Gibson-Hill pointed out that mariners sailing south from China towards the Java Sea ports on the north coast of Java would need to make landfall on the southwest coast of Kalimantan. However, mariners heading up the Strait of Melaka would make their way through or south of the Riau islands to head towards Bangka and up the Sungei Musi River to where Palembang is today, to call at Śrīvijaya, the primary emporium at the southern end of the Strait of Melaka from the seventh to the second half of the eleventh century, when the centre shifted to Jambi. As Gibson-Hill noted, there would have been no interest in seeking out the Strait of Singapore for sailing between the South China Sea and the Bay of Bengal for as long as Śrīvijaya was the preferred port-of-call polity at the southern end of the Strait of Melaka. It was only after Śrīvijaya declined, at the end of the twelfth century, that traders and mariners started searching for alternative waterways linking the South China Sea and the Bay of Bengal, and that the passages for sailing past Singapore came into use. The evidence recovered from some thirty-five years of archaeological investigations on Fort Canning confirms that Temasek was established towards this end, of serving sailors and traders sailing past its shores.

Gibson-Hill's main argument in his 1955 monograph was, however, that sailing past Singapore on any one of the four passages around the island (hugging the north coast of Singapore island to sail through the Johor Strait, hugging the south coast of Singapore and sailing through Keppel Harbour, sailing south of Sentosa on the Sisters Fairway past St John's Island, or taking the main strait) was always a hazardous event because of the numerous islets, shoals and coral reefs, and rapidly changing currents. Gibson-Hill argued that sailors and shippers had throughout the millennium a choice of which passage to take, and that choice was determined by their knowledge of the waterways and their seamanship to navigate the waters around Singapore. Most ship captains took onboard an *orang laut batin* or local sea nomad to pilot them through Singapore waters.

Fifty years were to pass before Peter Borschberg reviewed and expanded Gibson-Hill's insights with early modern European cartographic and other records—primarily Portuguese and Dutch—which were unavailable to Gibson-Hill in the 1950s.[13] Benjamin Khoo's essay is thus a useful update, summarizing what we know today about the challenges of sailing past Singapore.

Borschberg[14] also reconstructed from the seventeenth-century Dutch archives the search by the Dutch for a base for their new East India company, the Vereenigde Oost-Indische Compagnie (VOC). Cornelis Matelieff de Jonge, as commander of the second VOC expedition to the East Indies from 1605 to 1608, not only traded as far as Canton, but also tried to capture Melaka from the Portuguese and establish trade relations with the local authorities. Matelieff also searched for possible locations for an eventual VOC headquarters in the region. To this end, Matelieff started negotiations with the Johor sultan Raja Bongsu at his port-settlement up the Johor River at Batu Sawar for a plot of land on Singapore to set up a Dutch fort.

Matelieff realized, however, that Singapore was not the most suitable site for the VOC to locate its regional headquarters, comparing it unfavourably to a site on the north Java coast such as Banten or the old port of Jayakerta, among four other possible locations. As Matelieff reported,

> the rendezvous at Johor is unsuitable, because one cannot reach it at every time of the year. It is also unsuitable to navigate and sail to at all locations, and then there is the jealousy of the aforementioned king [of Johor] who does not want to concede us a fortress there…[15]

Two centuries later, Stamford Raffles assessed Singapore's location for a "British Station" rather differently.

The implication from Gibson-Hill's 1955 insights is that Singapore's fortunes as a British port-city, and earlier Temasek, depended to a large extent on what was happening on the sea in front of its harbours than we have hitherto acknowledged. Within a larger maritime context, it is primarily the structure and cycles of trade in the South China Sea and the Bay of Bengal that shaped the fortunes of Singapore as a port city. It depended also on the state of marine technology of shipbuilding, navigation and seamanship to sail to or through Singapore waters. Further, Singapore's fortunes have also been dependent upon how well it adapted to and networked with the maritime world it was a part of.

The Port City as the Cradle of Singapore's History

The "British Station" Raffles established on Singapore was linked with Penang and Melaka in 1826 to form the Straits Settlements. It was governed from the headquarters of the EIC in Calcutta until 1867, when control over the Settlements was transferred to London to become Crown Colonies until the end of World War II. However, underlying this constitutional framing of Singapore's history is a deeper history of Singapore as a port-polity.

Historian Tan Tai Yong argued in his 2019 IPS–Nathan Lectures[16] that,

Historically, Singapore functioned as a port thriving on flows of people and trading networks that stretched from the Persian Gulf to the southern coast of China. Today, Singapore positions itself as a hub for the greater Asian region and beyond. And I [Tan Tai Yong] would argue that the underlying plot of the Singapore story has not changed fundamentally throughout its history.

Tan quotes maritime historians Peter Reeves, Frank Broeze and Kenneth McPherson that "port cities are not merely 'cities that happen to be on the shoreline'; they are economic entities whose character is maritime in character". As Broeze and his colleagues stress, "the main economic base [of the port city] must be its port. Indeed, the port must become the central dynamic force and organizing principle of the port city, and not remain a 'hidden function', a mere appendage."[17] Port cities are, according to Broeze and his colleagues, in a telling phrase, "Brides of the Sea".

Within this context of port cities, Chinatown, Kampong Glam and Tanjong Pagar developed in response to the emergence of quays along the Singapore River, the harbour in the Kallang River and docks at Tanjong Pagar. The town plan Raffles drew up in 1822, as architectural historian Imran bin Tajudeen[18] argues, was an attempt to rationalize and plan the expanding "British Station" in line with other emerging port cities that Raffles had experienced—Penang, Melaka and the northern Javanese coastal cities. All these coastal cities, as Imran points out, were grounded on the morphology of earlier Malay port cities, the *negeri*.

The multi-ethnic community of itinerant and resident traders and others in Chinatown, Kampong Glam and Tanjong Pagar reflected the entrepôt trade of their quays, harbours and docks, where Asian and European trade networks interacted. Local and foreign cultural interactions produced a cosmopolitan culture that defined not only Singapore but also all other port cities and facilitated their networking.[19]

It was the bicentennial of the establishment by Raffles of a "British Station" on Singapore that prompted a review of Raffles's achievement in the long cycles of time and recognition that there were predecessor port settlements on Singapore in the fourteenth and sixteenth centuries.[20] As Prime Minister Lee Hsien Loong declared at the launch of the bicentennial commemoration on 28 January 2019,

> Today we mark a significant anniversary in Singapore's history. Stamford Raffles did not "discover" Singapore, any more than Christopher Columbus "discovered" America. By the time Raffles arrived in 1819, Singapore had already had hundreds of years of history. In the fourteenth century, this area, at the mouth of the Singapore River, was a thriving seaport called Temasek.

Raffles was certainly aware of an earlier settlement on Singapore, which he recognized as the "ancient capital of the Kings of Johor", and saw the remnants of its ruins. Archaeological excavations since 1984 have recovered several tonnes of artefacts attesting to a thriving port settlement in the fourteenth century around the environs of what is today Fort Canning. There was also another port settlement in the sixteenth century, which was probably located in the Kallang Estuary. Kwa Chong Guan's essay in this volume correlates the few textual and cartographic references to this port settlement in the European records with fragmentary archaeological evidence to argue for the existence of this forgotten port settlement.

Singapore's history begins with these pre-modern port cities and continues with the nineteenth-century quays, harbours and docks along the Singapore River and in the Kallang estuary, around which the town grew. From the mid-nineteenth century, a "New Harbour" was developed at Tanjong Pagar to cope with the expanding trade with the opening of the Suez Canal and the development of steamships. Today, that "New Harbour" has given way to a new mega port at Tuas with the infrastructure to handle the expanding containerization of commodities.

Underlying the expansion of old docks and wharves and the development of new harbours is the competition for land between bunkering services for shipping, ship repair and construction, and industry, banking and other businesses related to maritime trade. As with other contemporary port cities in Asia and around the world, Singapore's ports have grown, but port activities have gradually become overshadowed by the industrial, financial or service activities of a port city. The port has become "hidden"; relocated from the city's core to its periphery, becoming an appendage of a global city. The city rises to dominate the waterfront. Within this framework of port cities in transition, the future of Singapore, and other port cities, is the interrelationships, as sociologist Sharon Siddique states it, between the port and the city through the mediating feature of a common waterfront. The issue, as Siddique asks, is how to unite land and water worlds.[21]

The Maritime World That Made Singapore

A port is a haven for sailors and shippers; a place where traders from different trading zones—a hinterland or another port city—met to trade and exchange their goods. The two shipwrecks that Singapore archaeologically excavated in the eastern approaches to the Singapore Strait provide some insights into who the sailors, shippers and traders were who called, or would have called, at Singapore, and about the cargoes they were carrying. These two shipwrecks are the latest in a series of some thirty shipwrecks that have been archaeologically excavated off the coast of Vietnam, off the east coast of the Malay Peninsula, in the Java Sea and in the Philippines in the preceding three decades.

These two wrecks are the material evidence of maritime trade and its routes that connected the various port polities and port cities of an Asian maritime world that Singapore was, and continues to be, a part of. The early ninth-century Belitung wreck that Singapore acquired the cargo of, which is now exhibited in the Asian Civilisations Museum,[22] is one of the more spectacular shipwrecks excavated. The evidence of these shipwrecks confirms our reading of the classical texts (primarily the Chinese and Arabic) of evolving maritime trade routes connecting West Asian with South and East Asian ports over long cycles of time, creating distinct but connected trading networks, and worlds, in the Indian Ocean and the South China Sea.

The German geographer Ferdinand Freiherr von Richhofen's (1833–1905) idea of a "Maritime Silk Road" connecting Europe and China, complementing the overland Silk Road connecting Roman Europe with Han China, has today become a dominant narrative of global history.[23] Temasek was a late node in these long cycles of trade forming a "Maritime Silk Road".[24] The larger regional context for this emergence of Temasek as a port polity in the fourteenth century has been elaborated by Derek Heng.[25] The Temasek Wreck provides us, in Heng's analysis in his essay, an insight into the "international history" that framed Temasek's fourteenth-century emergence and decline.

The "British Station" Raffles established took off because an expanding British economy generated a consumer passion for things Chinese, in particular tea, and a "Chinamania" for blue-and-white porcelains. The EIC's royal charter gave it a monopoly of trade between Britain and China. But intra-Asian trade along the coast of India and between India and the East Indies, as Southeast Asia was then known, and onwards to China was in the hands of a group of private or country traders operating outside the Company's monopoly. Peter Borschberg, in his essay in this volume, examines the Company's relations with this group of traders who operated outside their jurisdiction. Many of these "country traders" were servants of the EIC who covertly carried out their personal trade on Company ships. The Company recognized by the late seventeenth century the reality of this covert trade by its servants on their vessels and decided to cut its losses by withdrawing from port-to-port trade in the East Indies and allowing its servants to engage in private trade, and in doing so the Company could reduce salaries to its staff.[26] The *Shah Muncher* Wreck is an example of the ships owned and operated by the country traders and the goods they traded in.

The relationship of the EIC with these country traders was symbiotic and complex, with each depending upon the other for their survival and profitability. It was a Madras-based country trader named Francis Light (1740–94) who persuaded the Company that it was in their (and the country trader's) interest to establish a base on Penang in 1786. The occupation of Melaka (1795), Dutch Java and the Maluku islands during the Napoleonic Wars (1803–1815) drew the Company willy-nilly deeper into the affairs of the East Indies, culminating in the establishment of the "British Station" on Singapore in 1819.

Equally, if not more important, was that the "British Station" on Singapore rose to prosperity on the tailwind of the Chinese junk trade from Amoy. The Hokkien junk traders brought to Singapore an extensive trading network reaching out from the southeastern Chinese port cities of Guangzhou and Quanzhou into the East and South China Seas.[27] This essentially Hokkien trading world is cartographically depicted in a singular seventeenth-century Chinese map that was donated to Oxford University's Bodleian Library by the English jurist and orientalist John Selden (1584–1654). The key feature of this Selden Map, as it has come to be known since its retrieval in 2008, lies in the sixty or more ports marked on its mapping of the South China Sea, and the sailing routes to these ports. The quays along the Singapore River were the heirs of the Hokkien trading world marked on this Selden Map. The Singapore River/Port, as Stephen Dobbs has argued, grew into a global emporium, behind which the town of Singapore developed.[28]

Local traders led by the Bugis[29] were another group of traders underpinning the development of Singapore into a port city. Disputes with the Dutch led the Bugis chieftain Arung Bellawa to bring some five hundred of his followers to Singapore in April 1820, where they were warmly welcomed and allocated settlement in the Kallang-Rochor area. The Bugis brought with them an extensive trading and shipping network, stretching from Makassar to the Riaus, dealing in local products, especially sea cucumbers or tripang, which were traded for firearms and gunpowder, parangs and other knives, and Indian and European textiles. So valuable was the Bugis trade that the Dutch tried to persuade Arung Bellawa to return to the Riaus.

The "British Station" Raffles established thrived as a trans-shipment centre and entrepôt for traders from the surrounding seas to call at and use as their base. It did not for its first half century have a hinterland in the Malay Peninsula, and was, as Tan Tai Yong[30] points out, "a port city in search of hinterlands", which it found in the late nineteenth century when Singapore became a financial, shipping and technology centre supporting the opening and development of the Malay Peninsula after British intervention in 1874. Like other Asian port cities, such as Bombay, Colombo, Batavia, Saigon and Rangoon, Singapore then became a beachhead for European colonial penetration into the hinterlands of their port cities.

Issues from the Shipwrecks for Our Understanding of Singapore's Maritime History

The Temasek Wreck and the *Shah Muncher* Wreck are, like all the other shipwrecks excavated, a kind of time capsule of the era in which they sank. The remains of their cargoes, other artefacts from the wreck and the fragments of the vessels reveal new insights into the nature of the trade these ships were engaged in, which is not often captured in the textual records. The 4.4 tonnes of Chinese ceramics recovered from the Temasek Wreck raises questions about our reconstruction and understanding of Temasek as an emporium. The *Shah Muncher* Wreck raises questions about the country traders who flocked to Singapore and made it their base.

The Temasek Wreck, like all other shipwrecks excavated—from the ninth-century Belitung Wreck to the *Shah Muncher*—carried large quantities of mass-produced Chinese ceramics.[31] The manifest of the *Shah Muncher* recorded that it was loaded with twenty tonnes of Chinaware on its return journey from China. But what is both unusual and significant about the cargo of the Temasek Wreck is, as Flecker points out, the unusually large quantity of underglaze blue-and-white ceramics compared with the ceramics recovered from the other contemporary wrecks he has either excavated or listed in his report. Blue-and-white ceramics—very common today—was an innovation in the fourteenth century when the Mongol empire connected West Asia with China and facilitated the transfer of the West Asian use of cobalt in glass and ceramic glazes to impart a bright blue colour to designs painted on the porcelains produced at the Chinese kilns at Jingdezhen.

Flecker infers that the unusually large quantities of these new blue-and-white wares on the ship suggests that Temasek, where it was likely headed, was a major regional entrepôt for the trade in Chinese ceramics. The recovery of significant quantities of similar blue-end-white wares in archaeological excavations on and around Fort Canning since 1984 suggests that Temasek was actively trading in blue-and-white porcelains and that the residents enjoyed a lifestyle that included using the newest products from China. Derek Heng's analysis in his essay confirms that the sociopolitical elites of Temasek residing on Fort Canning Hill were utilizing more blue-and-white ceramics than residents of Temasek living behind the wharves on the banks of the river, as would be expected.

The large cargo of Chinese porcelains on the Temasek Wreck (and many other wrecks) raises a fundamental issue about the nature of Asian trade. The Dutch historian J.C. van Leur[32] argued in his 1930 studies that Asian trade was, as in medieval Europe, essentially a small-scale peddling trade in which traders with their consignments of handicrafts and bags of pepper boarded a ship to trade at ports the ship would call at. Van Leur discounted bulk trade in low-value commodities, such as comestibles. This has been challenged by M.A.P. Meilink-Roelofsz,[33] who pointed out that Melaka—as described in the Portuguese records, especially by the Portuguese supervisor of its spice trade, Tomé Pires (not available to van Leur in the 1930s)—was heavily dependent upon the bulk trade in everyday staples, including rice, vegetables, sugar and fermented foods. The manifests we have found of sixteenth-century Asian ships inform us that traders—van Leur's "peddlers"—boarded ships not with a few bags of pepper, but with tonnes of pepper and other staples.

The large number of neatly bundled and stacked plates on board shipwrecks, from the enormous quantity of Changsha ware on the Tang dynasty Belitung to the Ming dynasty wrecks excavated off the coasts of Vietnam and peninsular Malaysia, confirms what Meilink-Roelofsz argued about trade at fifteenth-century Melaka—that it was not entirely a pedalling trade in the earlier era, but also involved trading in bulk. Extending that understanding of the nature of Asian trade suggests that the cargo of the Temasek Wreck (and other wrecks) represented wholesale trade of mass-produced ceramics involving large-scale financing. But who was responsible for financing this wholesale trade of the best and brightest products of the Jingdezhen kilns to Temasek?

Van Leur[34] provided some insight on this: in Asian ports, the ruler and aristocracy—as well as the (rich) merchants (*orang kaya*)—dominated the trade of their ports, imposing levies and tolls, and enforced stapling. In other words, Asian rulers of port polities may have, like their medieval European counterparts, practised a form of investing on *commenda*, in which they would invest or fund a trader or captain of a ship to trade on their behalf. Tomé Pires[35] provides a fairly clear description of Melaka's version of a *commenda*:

> If I am a merchant in Malacca and give you, the owner of the junk, a hundred cruzados of merchandise at the price then ruling in Malacca, assuming the risk myself, on the return they give me hundred and forty and nothing else; and the payment is made, according to the Malacca ordinance, forty-four days after the arrival of the junk in port.

Pires is here referring to the *Undang-Undang Melaka* (Laws of Melaka) on the "Rules on the Supplying of Capital to Someone":[36]

> [If] a provider of capital says to his agent: 'Take dinars [or] gold or silver and use it for business, the profit for you is such and such an amount", the profit derived from the sale [transaction] must be fixed beforehand. Meanwhile if the capital is lost or if there were losses, he [the agent]

need not be compensated for [the loss] of the business or the loss of the property [provided] it was not caused by any negligence on his part.

An earlier chapter of this *Undang-Undang Melaka* deals with the "rules governing [the] consignment" of valuables and other goods in the context of family affairs, but it would also be applicable to the consignment of trade goods between traders and their financiers. *Commenda* trade was, as Meilink-Roelofsz[37] has documented, practised by other sultans in the Indonesian archipelago.

The Dutch apparently found it useful to continue this local practice of *commenda*. Researcher Peter Potters has found in the VOC archives documents relating to the wreck Flecker[38] excavated off the coast of Binh Thuan Province. Among them is the *cedula* (legal agreement) that the VOC factor Victor Sprinckel, based at Patani, and one Hendrik Janssens concluded with the Chinese merchant Em Po, providing him with 410 elephant tusks for a return cargo of fine silk, with the Dutch merchants covering the risk of the outward and return voyages. The "respectable *orang kaya* Sirenarre Wanxsa" and Em Po were guarantors of this *cedula*. Flecker, in his essay on the *Shah Muncher* Wreck in this volume, has suggested a link between the Binh Thuan Shipwreck to a 21 July 1608 report by the VOC factor Abraham van den Broecke (based at Batu Sawar, up the Johor River), in which Broecke describes how he has "received news that I Sin Ho, the Chinese merchant, while returning with his junk [to Johor] was lost at sea somewhere about Cambodia. For that reason, the VOC loses 10 piculs of raw silk and other Chinese goods."

Was there some kind of *commenda* system in fourteenth-century Temasek? If so, who would have underwritten this order of Chinese ceramics for sale or redistribution in Temasek? Were the settlement's *rajas* and their *orang kaya* sufficiently wealthy to fund a trader to go to Jingdezhen, the City of Blue-and-White porcelain, to purchase this consignment of Chinese ceramics? Would this funding have been in some form of coinage, or silver? Or, perhaps more likely, as in the case of the Dutch-funded I Sin Ho, it could have been in valuable local produce, such as hornbill casques, lakawood and cotton prints, for which the fourteenth-century Quanzhou trader Wang Dayuan recorded Temasek to be a notable port of supply?

Further, how did fourteenth-century Temasek and other earlier and later harbour settlements deal with the arrival and distribution of these large cargoes of Chinese ceramics? The several tonnes of sherds of Chinese ceramics and local earthenware excavated from around Fort Canning suggest some system of storage, inventory control and distribution of these large volume of ceramics, earthenware and other cargoes, which we currently have no information on. At least for the nineteenth-century Singapore River we have the godowns along the quays as evidence of how goods were stored.

The *Shah Muncher*, which sank twenty-six years before Raffles arrived at Singapore, raises a different set of questions about the role of the country traders in the historical development of Singapore. Who were these country traders, who, from their base in the Indian port cities of Bombay, Calcutta or Madras, extended their trading networks into the port polities of the East Indies and on to Canton and Nagasaki? How did they interact with local rulers and conduct trade with them and other Asian traders, and in so doing open up new spheres of British commercial and political influence? How did they relate to the EIC who licensed them? Should the Company cooperate and work with these country traders, or hold them at arm's length, as the Company had no influence over them and their activities, which may not be in the Company's interest?[39]

Stamford Raffles, serving in Penang, would have interacted with the country traders. As a Company official he appeared to be ambivalent about country traders operating beyond the control of the Company. But he was aware of their resources, influence with the local rulers and knowledge of the region. Two of the six vessels making up the expedition by Raffles to find a suitable site for a British station at the southern end of the Strait of Melaka were country trader ships from Calcutta: the *Mercury*, owned by the trader J.R. Beaumont, and the *Indiana*, on which Raffles sailed, which belonged to James Pearl. Prior to this, Raffles had drawn extensively on information from country traders in planning the invasion of Java in 1811, and thereafter for the administration of British-occupied Java. Raffles also appeared to draw on information from country traders in Penang about the situation at the southern end of the Strait of Melaka in planning his expedition to search for a location for a British station in that vicinity.

The country trader Alexander Hamilton was aware of the significance of Singapore long before Raffles. He befriended the Bendahara sultan Abdul-Jalil while trading in Johor in 1703, and Hamilton records in his *Account of the East Indies* how the sultan "made me a present of the island of Singapura, but I told him it could be of no use to a private person tho' a proper place for a Company to set up a Colony on...". Hamilton was absolutely right that the Island of Singapore would have been of no use to him as an itinerant trader sailing from port to port. It fell to Raffles "to set up a colony on" Singapore 116 years later.

The establishment of a Company settlement on Singapore, and before that, at Melaka and Penang, provided the itinerant country trader the opportunity to put down some roots and become a resident merchant. Singapore, as a nineteenth-century port city, needed not only traders to call at its ports but also resident merchants with connections and lines of credit to the major agency houses in Calcutta and banks and insurers in London.[40] Dr John Crawfurd, as the second Resident of Singapore, reported that in 1824 "there are 12 European firms, either agents of or connected with good London or Calcutta houses".

Alexander Lauri Johnston, a former EIC mariner who owned and commanded his own vessel, was among the first country traders to establish his own company in Singapore, in 1819 or 1820. Johnston was a confidant of Raffles, who appointed him as a magistrate in 1823. Other country traders followed, either establishing their own companies or joining up with other merchants, like the China trader Thomas Harrington, who entered into a partnership with Alexander Guthrie.[41] This partnership ended in 1823, but the company Guthrie established went from trading and related services to become a major conglomerate in the plantation industry in the nineteenth and into the twentieth century, before then Malaysian prime minister Mahathir Mohammad moved to acquire the company on the London Stock Exchange.

The country traders thus contributed much to the success of the "British station" Raffles established. Ironically, the success of Singapore was also the death knell of the country trader. They could not compete with the Hokkien merchants, the Bugis-Makassar and other Southeast Asian traders in bringing in local products—from the pepper and nutmeg of the Moluccas to the tripang collected from the coral reefs of the Riaus—to Singapore for trans-shipment to China or Europe. Neither did they have the resources of the resident merchants representing the major agency houses in Calcutta to bring in the goods from India and England to be traded for the local produce, or the credit lines to finance that trade.

Concluding Reflections on the Maritime Dimension of Singapore History

In 2005, a group of maritime institutions led by the Singapore Shipping Corporation and the Maritime and Port Authority of Singapore, with the support of three other maritime institutions, sponsored a commemorative volume on the *Maritime Heritage of Singapore*, to which former president S.R. Nathan contributed an essay on seamen's unions. Tan Tai Yong, who contributed three essays to the volume, declared in his "Message" that "the Story of Singapore is essentially the story of the seas that surround it".[42]

The essays gathered in this volume explore how the two historic shipwrecks excavated in the eastern approach to the Strait of Singapore represent a significant addition to our maritime heritage, enhancing our awareness of how, as Tan wrote, "the Story of Singapore is essentially the story of the seas that surround it".

If the history of Singapore is about a journey towards nationhood, then that journey is about a port city developing into a global city, and is dependent on what was happening in the seas it was located in. As with all other port cities, from Quanzhou to Venice, the historical development of Singapore was very much dependent upon the monsoons and currents swirling around the port city, determining when and how ships could sail into and out of Singapore, the connectivity of shipping lanes on which ships sail, and its port facilities to attract traders and mariners. The challenge is how to connect Singapore's local, now national, history with a global history of the seas around Singapore. The sea is not only the stage on which Singapore's history was and is being played out, but, rather, happenings on the sea are the plot of Singapore's history.

Notes

1. Michael Flecker, *The Wreck of the* Shah Muncher *(1796), Singapore: Preliminary Report*, Temasek Working Paper Series no. 3 (Singapore: Temasek History Research Centre, ISEAS – Yusof Ishak Institute, 2022) and Michael Flecker, *The Temasek Wreck (mid-14th Century), Singapore – Preliminary Report*, Temasek Working Paper Series no. 4 (Singapore: Temasek History Research Centre, ISEAS – Yusof Ishak Institute, 2022).

2. John Crawfurd, *A Descriptive Dictionary of the Indian Islands & Adjacent Countries* (1856; repr., Kuala Lumpur: Oxford in Asia Historical Reprints, 1971), p. 402. Crawfurd compiled his *Dictionary* from his earlier reports and books when he retired in 1828. Crawfurd's *Dictionary* remains an authoritative summary of what was known about Southeast Asia in the nineteenth century.

3. On Dutch and British demarcation and policing of their maritime borders, see Eric Tagliacozzo, *Secret Trades, Porous Borders: Smuggling and States along a Southeast Asian Frontier, 1865–1915* (New Haven: Yale University Press, 2005).

4. Admiral Peter Rainier (1741–1808), commander of the Royal Navy in the Indian Ocean and the East from 1794 to 1805, established British dominance of the Indian Ocean against a renewed French challenge to British supremacy in India and the East Indies, with Britain taking over Holland's colonies in 1795. On this, see Peter Ward, *British Naval Power in the East 1794–1805: The Command of Admiral Peter Rainier* (Woodbridge: Boydell Press, 2013).

5. Wong Lin Ken, "The Strategic Significance of Singapore in Modern History", in *A History of Singapore*, edited by Ernest C.T. Chew and Edwin Lee (Singapore: Oxford University Press), p. 31.

6. Peter Borschberg, *The Singapore and Melaka Straits: Violence, Security and Diplomacy in the 17th Century* (Singapore: NUS Press, 2010), pp. 117–36.

7. C. Northcote Parkinson, *Trade in the Eastern Seas, 1793–1813* (Cambridge: University Press, 1937).

8. C. Northcote Parkinson, *War in the Eastern Seas 1793–1815* (London: Allen & Unwin, 1954)

9. In this respect Singapore was no different from its neighbours, especially the Philippines and Indonesia, whose struggles for independence were also for territory. These nations recognized belatedly the significance of the sea for their sovereign status and the need to resolve maritime disputes. Indonesia, for example, initially allowed the waters lying between their islands to be regarded as open seas, and only moved to claim "absolute sovereignty" over all the waters lying within straight baselines drawn between the outermost of its islands as an "archipelagic state " in 1957. See Vivian Forbes, *Conflict and Cooperation in Managing Maritime Space in Semi-enclosed Seas* (Singapore: Singapore University Press, 2001).

10. See Malcolm Murfett, *In Jeopardy: The Royal Navy and British Far Eastern Defence Policy, 1945–1951* (Kuala Lumpur: Oxford University Press, 1995) on why the Singapore naval base was rehabilitated and restored to something of its former glory after World War II.

11. Wong Lin Ken, "A View of Our Past", in *Singapore in Pictures, 1819–1945*, edited by Lee Yik and C.C. Chang (Singapore: Sin Chew Jit Poh and Ministry of Culture, 1981), p. 15.

12. Carl-Alexander Gibson-Hill, "Singapore Old Strait and New Harbour, 1300–1870" (1955), reprinted in *Studying Singapore before 1800*, edited by Kwa Chong Guan and Peter Borschberg (Singapore: NUS Press, 2018), pp. 221–308. I thank M. Flecker for pointing out to me issues in Gibson-Hill's understanding of sailing on the northeast monsoon in the South China Sea.

13. Peter Borschberg, "Remapping the Straits of Singapore? New Insights from Old Sources", in *Iberians in the Singapore-Melaka Area (16th to 18th Century)*, edited by Peter Borschberg (Wiesbaden: Harrassowitz, 2004), pp. 93–130.

14. Peter Borschberg, ed., *Admiral Matelieff's Singapore and Johor (1606–1616)* (Singapore: NUS Press, 2016), pp. 41–57.

15. Ibid., p. 155.

16. Tan Tai Yong, *The Idea of Singapore: Smallness Unconstrained* (Singapore: World Scientific, 2020), pp. 82–83.

17. Frank Broeze, ed., *Brides of the Sea: Port Cities of Asia from the 16th–20th Centuries* (Kensington, Australia: New South Wales University Press, 1989), p. 39. See also the follow-up volume, Frank Broeze, ed., *Gateways of Asia: Port Cities of Asia in the 13th–20th Centuries* (New York: Routledge, 1997).

18. Imran bin Tajudeen, "Reconsidering Raffles' Town Plan and its Position in the Urban History of Singapore and the Southeast Asian Port City", in *Raffles Revisited: Essays on Collecting and Colonialism in Java, Singapore, and Sumatra*, edited by Stephen Murphy (Singapore: Asian Civilisations Museum, 2021), pp. 148–79.

19. As displayed in the Asian Civilisations Museum. See Peter Lee et al., *Port Cities, Multicultural Emporiums of Asia 1500–1900* (Singapore: Asian Civilisations Museum, 2016).

20. On how the bicentennial of the arrival of Raffles at Singapore has been relocated in the long cycles of time, see Kwa Chong Guan, "The Singapore Bicentennial as Public History", *Journal of Southeast Asian Studies* 50, no. 4 (2019): 469–75.

21. Sharon Siddique, *Asian Port Cities: Uniting Land and Water Worlds*, compiled by Sharon Siddique and Shanty G. Coomaraswamy (Singapore: Lee Kuan Yew Centre for Innovative Cities, 2016).

22. For a catalogue of the Belitung Wreck exhibition, see Alan Chong and Stephen Murphy, eds. *The Tang Shipwreck: Art and Exchange in the 9th Century* (Singapore: Asian Civilisations Museum, 2017).

23. Kwa Chong Guan, *The Maritime Silk Road: History of an Idea*. Nalanda-Sriwijaya Centre Working Paper no. 23 (2016), pp. 2–13.

24. For a reconstruction of the cycles of trade and the trading worlds of this Maritime Silk Road, see Roderich Ptak, *Die Maritime Seidenstraße, Küstenräume, Seefahrt und Handel in vorkolonialer Zeit* (Munich: Beck, 2007).

25. Derek Heng, "Situating Temasik within the Larger Regional Context: Maritime Asia and Malay State Formation in the Pre-modern Era", in *Singapore in Global History*, edited by Derek Heng and Syed Muhd Khairudin Aljunied (Amsterdam: Amsterdam University Press, 2011), pp. 27–50.

26. W.G. Miller, *British Traders in the East Indies, 1770-1820: "At Home in the Eastern Seas"* (Woodbridge, Suffolk: Boydell, 2020).

27. Kwa Chong Guan, "Prelude to the History of the Chinese in Singapore", in *A General History of the Chinese in Singapore*, edited by Kwa Chong Guan and Kua Bak Lim (Singapore: World Scientific/Singapore Federation of Chinese Clan Associations, 2019), pp. 3–20.

28. Stephen Dobbs, "The Singapore River/Port in a Global Context", in *Singapore in Global History*, edited by Derek Heng and Syed Muhd Khairudin Aljunied (Amsterdam: Amsterdam University Press, 2011), pp. 51–66.

29. Glenn Hamonic, "The Bugis-Makassar Merchant Networks: The Rise and Fall of the Principle of the Freedom of the Seas", in *Asian Merchants and Businessmen in the Indian Ocean and the China Sea*, edited by Denys Lombard and Jean Aubin (New Delhi: Oxford University Press, 2000), pp. 256–59.

30. Tan, *The Idea of Singapore*, pp. 83–113, esp. fn. 16.

31. See Kwa Chong Guan, *Locating Singapore on the Maritime Silk Road: Evidence from Maritime Archaeology, Ninth to Early Nineteenth Centuries*. Nalanda-Sriwijaya Centre Working Paper no. 10 (2012), which contains an inventory of the major shipwrecks that have been archaeologically excavated.

32. Jacob Cornelis van Leur, *Indonesian Trade and Society: Essays in Asian Social and Economic History* (The Hague and Bandung: van Hoeve, 1955).

33. Marie Antoinette Petronella Meilink-Roelofsz, Asian *Trade and European Influence in the Indonesian Archipelago between 1500 and about 1630* (The Hague: Nijhoff, 1962).

34. Van Leur, *Indonesian Trade and Society*, p. 133.

35. Armando Cortesão, ed. *The Suma Oriental of Tomé Pires: An Account of the East, from the Red Sea to Japan, Written in Malacca and India in 1512–1515* (Hakluyt Society, 1944; repr., New Delhi: Asian Educational Services, 1990), p. 284.

36. Liaw Yock Fang, *Undang-Undang Melaka: The Laws of Melaka* (The Hague: Nijhoff, 1976), p. 147.

37. Meilink-Roelofsz, *Asian Trade and European Influence*, pp. 48–52. For a more recent overview of systems and structures of trade in the fifteenth to seventeenth centuries, see Anthony Reid, *Southeast Asia in the Age of Commerce, 1450–1680*, vol. 2, *Expansion and Crisis* (New Haven: Yale University Press, 1993), pp. 64–131.

38. Michael Flecker, "The Binh Thuan Wreck (Containing the Complete Archaeological Report)", in *Christie's Australia: The Binh Thuan Shipwreck* (Melbourne: Christie's, 2004). See also Flecker's essay on the *Shah Muncher* Wreck in this volume.

39. These issues of how to relate to private or country traders was not specific to the English EIC. The VOC also tried to restrict a number of their senior officers from engaging in personal trade. This issue of private trade was sufficiently significant to be raised to the board of directors of the VOC, the Gentlemen XVII, several times in the course of the seventeenth century, as noted by its long-serving secretary and senior advocate Pieter van Dam (1621–1706). On this, see J. de Hulla, "Een advise van mr. Pieter van Dam, advocaat der Oost-Indische Compagnie, over een geeltelijke openstelling van compagnie's handel voor particulieren, 1662", *Bijdragen tot de Taal-, Land- en Volkenkunde* 73, no. 1 (1918): 267–98. It would appear the Dutch also tried to restrict English country traders, causing issues and tensions between the Companies.

40. Peter Drake, *Merchants, Bankers, Governors: British Enterprise in Singapore and Malaya, 1786–1920* (Singapore: World Scientific, 2018), pp. 1–24.

41. Sjovald Cunyngham-Brown, *The Traders: A Story of Britain's South-East Asian Commercial Adventure* (London: Newman Neame, 1971).

42. Aileen Lau and Laure Lau, eds., *Maritime Heritage of Singapore* (Singapore: Suntree Media, 2005). S.R. Nathan's essay recollects his early career as a social welfare officer assigned to work with seamen's unions.

2

The Temasek Wreck

Michael Flecker

The fourteenth-century Temasek Wreck was excavated recently off Pedra Branca by the Archaeology Unit (AU) of the ISEAS – Yusof Ishak Institute (ISEAS) on behalf of the Singapore National Heritage Board (NHB). Details of the discovery, survey, excavation and outcomes are provided in the ISEAS publication Temasek Working Paper Series no. 4.[1] Key findings, such as the cargo composition, date of loss, likely origin of the ship, probable port of lading and most likely destination are presented here, but not as stand-alone outcomes. The aim is to place the Temasek Wreck within the context of contemporary shipwrecks in this region in order to better understand the significance of early Singapore in the realm of regional maritime trade.

The Temasek Wreck

The Temasek Wreck was excavated intermittently from 2016 until 2019. Approximately 3.5 tonnes of ceramics were recovered, but little else. The ship itself had completely vanished. Without the anaerobic protection of deep and fine sediments, the hull has been scattered by waves and currents and consumed by *Teredo* worms.

Figure 2.1 A scuba diver uses an airlift to excavate Grid F20 at the Temasek Wreck site. (ISEAS)

While some intact examples have been retrieved, most of the ceramics are in the form of shards. Stoneware storage jars and small-mouth jars—most likely from Cizao—Longquan celadon dishes, bowls and jars and *qingbai* ware from Jingdezhen form the vast majority. There are small quantities of crude Fujian greenware, Dehua whiteware and fine *shufu* ware. But the most impressive element of the ceramic cargo is an extensive repertoire of rare Yuan dynasty blue-and-white porcelain, far more than has ever been recovered from a documented wreck site anywhere else in the world.

Without dated coins or organic material suitable for radiocarbon analysis, dating can only be attempted through the stylistic analysis of the ceramics cargo.

Longquan celadon first appeared in the twelfth century. It was favoured throughout most of the thirteenth century by the Song imperial court for its sumptuous jade-like attributes. During the fourteenth century, the Longquan kilns expanded production to cater to an ever-increasing demand for a wide repertoire of large moulded shapes from domestic and foreign markets. The array of Longquan celadon recovered from the Temasek Wreck is typical of the fourteenth century, but being more specific can be contentious due to the longevity of various decorative techniques and patterns. In the later part of the fourteenth century, jade-like glazes gave way to unctuous sea green and glassy pea green.[2] However, subtle differences in hue could be the result of firing variations or chemical attack on the seabed, precluding such observations from refining a production date for the celadon cargo from the Temasek Wreck.

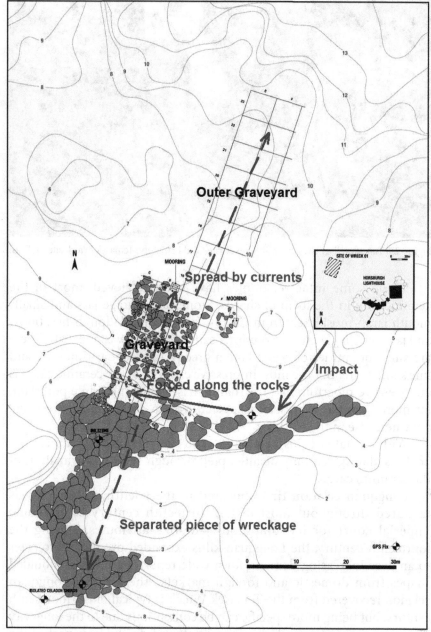

Figure 2.2 The Temasek Wreck site excavation grid layout and bathymetry, with a depiction of the wrecking process. (Adapted from a schematic diagram by Aaron Kao.)

The Yuan dynasty spanned the years 1271 to 1368. It is during this period of Mongol rule that blue-and-white porcelain was first commercially produced in the kilns of Jingdezhen, utilising cobalt imported from Persia. While the finest pieces were reserved for the emperor and nobility, the rest was available for export. The exported wares were still of exceptional quality, and surviving pieces are now prized the world over.

While Yuan blue-and-white porcelain has been studied extensively by archaeologists, ceramicists and art historians, there is still no consensus on the earliest date of production, which ranges from 1323 to the early 1330s. The predominant motif on the Temasek Wreck blue-and-white lends itself to more precise dating. The Wenzong Emperor's signature motif, reserved for his exclusive use from 1328 to 1332, was water birds, typically mandarin ducks, in a lotus pond. In 1340, when the Shundi (Zhizheng) Emperor assumed full power, restrictions on the use of this motif probably ceased. This led to private kilns making a flood of wares decorated in this manner, with many intended for export.[3]

The invasion of the Red Turban Army, made up of rebels aiming to oust the Mongol rulers, shut down the imperial kilns in Jingdezhen for an extended period from 1352. From archaeological evidence, there is a strong possibility that all of the Jingdezhen kilns were forced to cease

Figure 2.3 After removal of overlying sediments, two Longquan dishes are revealed, adjacent to a blue-and-white stem-bowl. (ISEAS)

operations.[4] The "ducks in a lotus pond" motif features prominently on Yuan blue-and-white porcelain in China, Southeast Asia, India, the Middle East and the Maghreb—an extraordinary distribution in both quantity and range in only twelve years. Perhaps some of the Jingdezhen kilns struggled on through the conflict.

The Yuan dynasty came to an end in 1368. In 1371, Ming emperor Hongwu ruled that foreign trade was only to be conducted through official tribute missions. Bulk cargoes of ceramics could no longer be exported. Consequently, a conservative date range for the Temasek Wreck is between 1340 and 1371. But there remains a distinct possibility that the remarkably tight date range of 1340 to 1352 applies. Either range places the wreck at the zenith of the Temasek period, when the Singapore River and the immediate hinterland played host to a dominant Southeast Asian port-city.

The key ports in southern China during the fourteenth century were Guangzhou in Guangdong province, Amoy (Xiamen), Quanzhou and Fuzhou in Fujian province, and Wenzhou, Ningbo and Hangzhou in Zhejiang province. With the ceramic cargo on the Temasek Wreck originating from the provinces of Fujian, Zhejiang and Jiangxi, the long-established trade centre of Quanzhou is perhaps the most likely port of lading, although diverse ceramic cargoes could have been loaded at various ports courtesy of an extensive riverine and coastal feeder network.

Remarkably, many of the Temasek Wreck finds have direct parallels to those unearthed during thirty years of terrestrial excavations in Singapore. The prevalent "mandarin ducks in a lotus pond" and the popular "lotus bouquet" motifs on the shipwreck blue-and-white porcelain are replicated on finds from Fort Canning, as are Longquan bowls with everted rims and carved lotus petals, and others with impressed twin fish or lotus flowers in the centre. Large Longquan celadon plates occur both on the wreck and at the Empress Place site. Longquan moulded jarlets of the type found on the shipwreck were also excavated at the National Gallery site. Dark blue glass beads and tiny fragments of gold foil show up both on the wreck and at Fort Canning. While a black glass bangle from the Temasek Wreck appears to be very different from a multicoloured glass bangle found at Fort Canning, the style is evidently the same. Both have a flat interior with a lip, a rounded exterior decorated with appliqué white glass dots, and are small, with an outside diameter of less than six centimetres. Unsurprisingly, more common ceramics such as storage jars and stoneware small-mouth jars occur on both the wreck and at most Singapore terrestrial sites.

It is clear therefore that ships with very similar cargoes to that of the Temasek Wreck regularly called at Temasek. Why then would the

Figure 2.4
Just excavated, an intact Longquan celadon dish with a foliated rim and a moulded floral motif in the centre. (ISEAS)

Figure 2.5
A Yuan blue-and-white porcelain bowl with the "mandarin ducks in a lotus pond" motif. (ISEAS)

Temasek Wreck, carrying a cargo known to have been in local demand, bypass this readily accessible thriving entrepôt? Temasek would have been in clear view to any ship passing through the Singapore Strait. Even for those intending to voyage further west, no course deviation would be required to stop off to trade and/or revictual.

The argument can be taken further. When making comparisons, sometimes a missing element can be more important than the common. The most famous ancient collections of Yuan blue-and-white porcelain occur in Turkey, the Middle East and India. Substantial quantities have been found at archaeological sites in Thailand, the Philippines and Indonesia, particularly at Trowulan in eastern Java. All have examples of

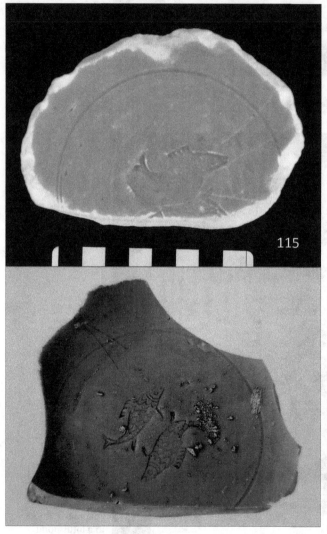

Figure 2.6
A Longquan celadon bowl with an impressed twin-fish motif from the Temasek Wreck (*top*; ISEAS), and a nearly identical piece found at Fort Canning, Singapore (*bottom*; courtesy of the National Parks Board and John Miksic).

large blue-and-white dishes with a diameter of 40 to 50 centimetres. In fact, those tend to be in the majority in the larger collections. While the undocumented Red Sea Wreck relinquished only twenty-one ceramic pieces, two thirds of them were large blue-and-white dishes.

So far, Singapore's terrestrial excavations have not revealed any large Yuan blue-and-white dishes. The Temasek ship carried a wide variety of Yuan blue-and-white wares, but there are only a few dishes, and the largest are less than 35 centimetres in diameter. The direct implication is that the Temasek ship was not destined for trade ports on the Indian Ocean littoral. With no Yuan blue-and-white finds in northern Sumatera or along the eastern shores of the Melaka Strait and the Bay of Bengal, Temasek would seem to be the only contender as a destination port. The cargo of the Temasek Wreck, including Chinese iron, was not intended for ports further west.

The oblique implication of the lack of large plates is that the blue-and-white cargo was intended for wealthy Temasek residents, and not necessarily for trans-shipment at all. If this is indeed the case, the recovered ceramics and artefacts provide an incredible insight into the utilitarian, elite and ceremonial wares that were used by the inhabitants.

Without any surviving hull remains, it is impossible to identify conclusively the origin of the Temasek Wreck. But it is possible to make a very good guess, calling upon archaeological evidence for the period. While exclusively Chinese cargoes were carried by several non-Chinese vessel types, there are always non-Chinese artefacts, such as personal possessions or objects for shipboard use, recovered from such wreck

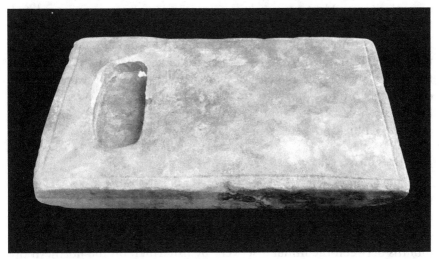

Figure 2.7 A utilitarian Chinese inkstone (14 x 8.5 cm). Chisel marks can be readily discerned on the reverse. (ISEAS)

sites. Chinese junks with exclusively Chinese cargoes, on the other hand, did not carry non-Chinese objects. Very few non-ceramic artefacts remained on the Temasek Wreck: an ink stone, tiny glass beads, a glass bangle, gold foil, lead disks, copper alloy vessel fragments and spoons, and a lead sinker. The ink stone is Chinese. At this stage, the origin of the other artefacts has not been confirmed, but there is nothing to suggest that they did not come from China. There is therefore a high probability that the ship was a Chinese junk.

Contemporary Shipwrecks

With the necessarily speculative identification of the Temasek Wreck, an analysis of other fourteenth-century shipwrecks found in the waters of East and Southeast Asia can provide a degree of corroboration. Indeed, these contemporary wrecks also provide context for the port of Temasek. The important shipwreck finds are paralleled, and sometimes overshadowed, by the wealth of material that has been excavated from terrestrial sites in Singapore. Heavily laden ships, exemplified by the various shipwreck types, traded with Temasek throughout the fourteenth century.

Sinan Wreck

The Sinan Wreck was found in Korean waters in 1975.[5] Researchers have concluded that the vessel was a Chinese junk originally destined for Japan. It has been precisely dated to 1323 by legible script on wooden cargo tags. Apart from twenty-eight tonnes of Chinese copper coins and a wide variety of artefacts, the wreck contained over twenty thousand ceramic items. Most were celadon wares from Longquan or related kilns in Zhejiang, with some being of exceptional quality. Other wares originated from various kilns in Fujian and from Jingdezhen. But, unlike the Temasek Wreck, there was no blue-and-white porcelain in the cargo. Such is the paucity of evidence for the earliest production of Jingdezhen blue-and-white that the date of the Sinan Wreck is cited by some scholars as the production *terminus post quem* because of the absence of blue-and-white from this otherwise rich cargo.

Jade Dragon Wreck

The Jade Dragon Wreck has been named after the most prized artefacts recovered from the site—jade-coloured Longquan celadon plates with a central appliqué dragon motif.[6] Most of the cargo consisted of Longquan celadon, but much of that unfortunately was looted in the three short months between the initial discovery by fishermen off the northern tip of Sabah, East Malaysia, and the commencement of an archaeological survey.

Figure 2.8
Part of a Longquan dish with an appliqué dragon from the Temasek Wreck (*top*) and a similar intact dish from the Jade Dragon Wreck. (ISEAS)

The celadon was of high quality and consisted of large and small plates, bowls, jarlets and guan-type jars. Apart from the few dragons, the large plates were mostly decorated with floral designs, while small plates tended to be decorated with appliqué twin fish. Other ceramic types included green-glazed kendi from Cizao, brownware jars from Cizao or kilns in Guangdong, and a few brown-on-white decorated shards from Cizhou. Again, there were no blue-and-white ceramics in the cargo.

Surviving planks, incorporating carved lugs and holes for edge-joining with dowels, confirm that the ship was of the Southeast Asian lashed-lug tradition. From the cargo and wreck location, she was perhaps bound from Wenzhou in China to Brunei or elsewhere on the northwest coast of Borneo.

Longquan plates with appliqué twin fish are generally attributed to the Southern Song, suggesting a late thirteenth-century wreck date. The twin fish decoration on some Longquan plates from the Temasek Wreck are impressed rather than appliqué.

Turiang Wreck

The Turiang Wreck was located some hundred nautical miles northeast of the Singapore Strait, forty-three metres beneath the South China Sea.[7] Bulkheads, iron fastenings, the absence of dowel edge-joining, and the identification of pine, a temperate timber species, implies that the ship was a Chinese junk. The ship carried a wide variety of ceramics: Sukhothai, Si-Satchanalai and Suphanburi wares from Thailand; underglaze iron decorated wares from Vietnam; green and brown glazed wares from Guangdong; and celadon from Longquan, China. Brown has dated this wreck from between 1370 and 1400 through the stylistic analysis of the ceramic cargo.[8] The lack of blue-and-white porcelain in the cargo may be explained by the curtailed production of the Jingdezhen kilns from 1371, when Ming Emperor Hongwu ruled that all foreign trade was to be conducted only through official tribute missions.

Dalian Island Wreck

Dalian Island is located at the northern entrance of the Haitan Strait, Pingtan County, Fujian province, China.[9] The wreck that takes its name from this nearby feature was excavated in 2006 and 2007. It yielded a cargo of Longquan celadon, along with some earthenware and iron artefacts. The Longquan forms included plates, bowls and jarlets variously decorated with flowers, dragons, fish, birds and figures. There was no blue-and-white porcelain on board.

It is assumed that the wreck is a Chinese junk. Researchers speculate that the ship departed from either Fuzhou or Wenzhou and was bound for a port in Southeast Asia. The attributed dating is mid to late Yuan dynasty. However, appliqué twin-fish plates and the lack of blue-and-white porcelain may be more indicative of early Yuan.

Binh Chau Wreck

In 2012, fishermen discovered a wreck just fifty metres off the beach near Binh Chau, Quang Ngai province, central Vietnam. As often occurs, there was much looting before police stepped in to protect the site. The wreck was particularly vulnerable, in water less than four metres deep. The provincial government quickly appointed a commercial salvage company to carry out an excavation on an artefact-sharing basis. In a bold move, the wreck was encircled by a sheet-pile cofferdam so that it could be excavated dry.

While there do not seem to be any archaeological reports published, photos in the press clearly show the characteristics of a Chinese junk: bulkheads with adjacent frames, occasional vertical "stiffeners" and even a collapsed mast with a tabernacle mast-step. Over five thousand artefacts are reported to have been salvaged—almost all ceramics. The ship carried Longquan celadon, mostly in the form of plates, but there were also jarlets and incense burners. The plates were decorated with flowers, fish, deer and dragons. Greenware of lesser quality originated from Fujian kilns. Brown-glazed jars and basins were probably from Guangdong. The few pieces of blue-and-white porcelain were clearly made at the Jingdezhen kilns, and are consistent with Yuan dynasty production. They are in the form of bowls, cups, dishes and a disproportionately large number of intact lids with the well-known tendril decoration.

Shiyu II Wreck

In 2010, Chinese archaeologists discovered and partially excavated a shipwreck site in the Paracels, a series of islands and reefs to the southeast of Hainan.[10] The site was located in clear shallow water on the eastern extremity of Observation Bank, just north of Drummond Island, in the Crescent Group. Not surprisingly in this exposed, typhoon-prone area, none of the hull timbers survived, and the ceramics cargo was fragmented and scattered far and wide. Extensive looting has added to the destruction. Of the 405 shards recovered during the official excavation, 103 were blue-and-white porcelain from Jingdezhen, which could be confidently dated to the Yuan dynasty. It is therefore the first— and, so far, only—discovery of Yuan blue-and-white porcelain on a wreck site in offshore Chinese waters.

The blue-and-white shapes include bowls, cups, vases, small-mouth jars (*meiping*), jarlets, kendis, pots and lids. The "ducks on a lotus pond" motif is the most common. There were also floral motifs, flames and the character *shou* (longevity).

Unlike the cargo of the Temasek Wreck, there were no Longquan celadons. Most of the non-blue-and-white ceramics are quite crude, coming from a variety of Fujian kilns and probably intended for the Southeast Asian utilitarian market. Less crude ceramics were produced in several other regions: whitewares from the kilns of Dehua, greenwares from Cizao, small-mouth jars from Cizao, and brownware storage jars perhaps from Guangdong.

Bracketing Shipwrecks

Casting the net wider, some of the shipwrecks bracketing the fourteenth century also have relevance. Considering a number of terrestrial ceramic finds that may be products of the Southern Song—and the iconic inscribed Singapore stone—the Temasek period perhaps commenced in the thirteenth century. And with the shift of power to Melaka at the end of the fourteenth century, Temasek did not suddenly disappear. Rather, it was relegated to subsidiary-port status.

Quanzhou Wreck

The Quanzhou Wreck is extremely important as it is the only documented example of a Chinese junk returning from the Nanhai.[11] She sank in a harbour around 1273 with a cargo of Southeast Asian commodities such as fragrant wood and cowrie shells, along with samples of ambergris, cinnabar, betel nuts, pepper and tortoise shell. The hull remains are 24 metres long and 9 metres wide. Twelve bulkheads are fastened to the hull planking by metal brackets and large frames. The hull planking itself is multilayered in complex clinker-like steps.

Ko Si Chang II Wreck

Brown gives a broad date range of 1370 to 1424 for this wreck based on the few ceramics found at the looted site.[12] They included Thai Sawankhalok, Sukhothai and Suphanburi wares and Chinese greenware. Partly as a result of trawling, only portions of the vessel structure survived, including sections of a double-planked hull and bottom planks fastened together with wooden pegs and metal nails.[13] Green comments extensively on plank edge-joining with diagonally driven iron nails but does not mention dowels at all.[14] This suggests the Ko Si Chang II Wreck is a Chinese junk.

Bakau Wreck

This wreck was found off Bakau Island on the western side of the Karimata Strait, Indonesia.[15] It contained a wide variety of ceramics from Thailand, China and Vietnam, including many huge Thai storage jars with organic contents. The hull remains were 23 metres long and 7 metres wide, and they displayed all the features typical of Chinese junk construction: bulkheads, adjacent frames, iron-nail edge-joining, wood stiffeners, chu-nam caulking and hull timbers of pine. She was flat-bottomed—the first and, so far, only example of such hull design found in a sea-going context (flat-bottomed junks are usually associated with coastal or riverine transport). The wreck has been dated to the early fifteenth century through carbon dating, stylistic analysis of ceramics, and Yongle (1403–24) coins found on board, making her contemporary with Zheng He's voyages.

Rang Kwien Wreck

The Rang Kwien Wreck was excavated by the Thai Fine Arts Department from 1978 to 1981 after it had been heavily looted. The wreck contained several tonnes of Chinese copper coins, with the most recent attributable to the Hongwu reign (1368–98). Of the few remaining ceramics, some fifty per cent consisted of earthenware, possibly Thai. About a quarter were Vietnamese underglaze blue- or blackwares. Only ten per cent were Chinese ceramics, with half of those being stoneware storage jars and the rest being crude greenwares. The balance consisted of Sawankhalok wares, a few Thai storage jars and three shards of Chinese blue-and-white porcelain. Brown is of the opinion that two of the blue-and-white shards are intrusive to the site, apparently being of a considerably later date than the rest of the ceramics.[16] From the coin dates and the stylistic analysis of the ceramic cargo, Brown gives this wreck a date range of 1400 to 1430.

Little coherent structure remained. There were no bulkheads evident, and the hull planks were edge-joined with dowels. According to Prishanchit, the hull planks were fastened to the frames with "round headed wooden pegs".[17] If this was indeed the case, the ship could be an early (and so far only) example of a Southeast Asian *jong*, where dowels have replaced the *ijok* lashings of the traditional lashed-lug hull. Enigmatically, it has been reported that a Chinese mirror was embedded in the keel.

Longquan Wreck

The Longquan Wreck was located in 63 metres of water, well offshore between Terengganu and Kuantan on the east coast of peninsular Malaysia. The hull measured more than 30 metres in length and 8 metres in width. She is of the South China Sea tradition. The site was destroyed by trawlers before a full excavation could take place. But a rough estimate suggests 40 per cent Chinese celadon from Longquan and other southern kilns, 20 per cent Thai Sukhothai underglaze decorated ware, and 20 per cent Thai Sawankhalok greenware. The tentative date range is given as 1424 to 1440.[18]

Nanyang Wreck

The Nanyang Wreck was found in 1995 at a depth of 54 metres east of Pulau Pemanggil, off the east coast of peninsular Malaysia. The ship is estimated to be 18 metres long by 5 metres wide, which is relatively small. Construction features include transverse bulkheads and dowel edge-joined planks, which are both characteristic of the South China Sea tradition. The primary cargo is Thai greenware from the Sisatchanalai kilns. The tentative date of the Nanyang Wreck is thought to range between 1425 and 1450, just slightly later than the Longquan Wreck.[19]

Discussion

From their location alone, it is evident that the Sinan, Jade Dragon and Bakau wrecks were not destined for Temasek.

The Sinan ship was a Chinese junk bound for Japan, while the Jade Dragon ship was a Southeast Asian lashed-lug ship bound for Brunei or another port on the northwest coast of Borneo. However, both ships carried ceramic cargoes dominated by Longquan celadon, a product that also characterizes Singapore terrestrial sites, so both are contenders for past or unrealized voyages to early Temasek.

The Bakau junk was almost certainly destined for Java, but it did not sail directly from China. The heavy Thai storage jars full of liquid or organic trade commodities suggest that an entrepôt such as Ayutthaya was one port of lading. While there were Chinese ceramics on board, the larger Thai and Vietnamese component would seem to discount Temasek as a destination for a cargo of this mix. Fifteenth-century cargoes of this nature, however, probably made their way through the Singapore Strait on Chinese junks destined for Melaka. This flat-bottomed junk, perhaps from northern China, also illustrates that various types of junk voyaged to Southeast Asian ports, quite likely including Temasek.

The Quanzhou junk was returning from Southeast Asia. It is feasible that she loaded all or part of her cargo of jungle and sea products at the fledgling port of Temasek. The original sources of the diverse cargo would have been as varied as the cargo itself, hence the need for an entrepôt.

All the other wrecks were en route to the Malay Peninsula or insular Indonesia, although the Dalian Island junk, with its almost exclusive cargo of Longquan celadon, may have been bound for Quanzhou or Guangdong on a feeder voyage. It may also have been bound directly for Temasek, as the cargo is consistent with terrestrial finds.

Given the dearth of Thai and Vietnamese wares unearthed from Temasek terrestrial sites, the Turiang, Ko Si Chang II, Rang Kwien, Longquan and Nanyang wrecks were unlikely to have had Temasek as their intended destination. The ships themselves, consisting of Chinese junks, South China Sea Tradition vessels of Siamese origin and a possible Southeast Asian *jong*, could all have traded with Temasek during earlier voyages, assuming that they were opportunistic and did not adhere to a single trade route.

This leaves the Binh Chau and Shiyu II wrecks as serious contenders for an intended visit to Temasek during their last voyage. Interestingly, both carried Yuan blue-and-white porcelain. The Binh Chau Wreck is a Chinese junk that also carried Longquan celadon and brown-glazed stoneware. Its location in only four metres of water very close to shore, in the region of the first landfall after departing from southern China, suggests it had stopped to trade and/or revictual. The surviving cargo is not particularly diverse, and the blue-and-white porcelain is of relatively low quality. The Shiyu II Wreck offers minimal remnants, but they are telling. Fujian trade wares, Dehua whitewares and stoneware small-mouth jars are typical of Temasek terrestrial finds. As is the range of blue-and-white porcelain, consisting mostly of small and medium sized shapes, with "ducks on a lotus pond" as one of the main motifs.

Conclusions

As stated at the outset, the aim of this chapter is to place the Temasek Wreck within the context of contemporary shipwrecks in order to better understand the significance of nearby Temasek in the realm of regional maritime trade. In doing so, it becomes evident that a range of vessel types carried a range of cargo types all over the South China Sea. There were Chinese junks, Southeast Asian lashed-lug craft, *jongs* and South China Sea Tradition ships. Some may have been bound for Temasek when they sank. Others may have called at Temasek during earlier voyages.

Some carried spectacular cargoes of high-quality ceramics—most notably the Sinan Wreck. Our perception may be distorted by the large quantity of glistening intact ceramics recovered from this site. While considerably smaller, the Jade Dragon Wreck would also have carried a high-quality cargo of Longquan celadon. But the wrecking process and looting have left us with eroded shards and only a handful of intact pieces. Many of the other wrecks relinquished considerable quantities of intact ceramics, but the quality cannot compare with the Sinan finds.

The Temasek Wreck yielded approximately 3.5 tonnes of ceramic shards and only a dozen or so fully intact pieces. And yet the quality of the ceramics is in many cases superlative. This is especially the case for the blue-and-white porcelain. Apart from large plates, items from the best collections throughout the world are represented on this wreck. There are guan-type jars with monster-head handles, octagonal guan, flasks, bowls, large bowls, vases, dishes, cups, stem-cups, stem-bowls, jars and jarlets. Motifs include the prevalent "ducks in a lotus pond" and lotus bouquets, dragons, phoenixes, herons, hares, and melons and vines, all in vibrant and multi-hued blues.

Besides the blue-and-white porcelain, Longquan celadon, stoneware storage jars, *qingbai* ware from Jingdezhen, whiteware from Dehua and small-mouth-jars from Cizao replicate the Temasek terrestrial finds. Had all the contemporary wrecks discussed above been judged on the likelihood of being destined for Temasek based on their surviving cargo alone, the Temasek Wreck would have won hands down. When the location of the wreck is considered, along with the dearth of large blue-and-white dishes, there can be little doubt.

In the process of placing the port of Temasek in the context of regional shipping, we have inadvertently tied the Temasek Wreck, which was initially named for the era, even closer to her namesake.

Figure 2.9
An intact blue-and-white porcelain bottle from the Temasek Wreck. It may be a surahi, an early hookah base or even a holy water container. It is thought to be the only one of its type in the world. (Photo courtesy of the Asian Civilisations Museum)

Notes

1. Michael Flecker, *The Temasek Wreck (mid-14th Century), Singapore – Preliminary Report*, Temasek Working Paper Series no. 4 (Singapore: ISEAS – Yusof Ishak Institute, 2022).

2. Laurie E. Barnes, "Yuan Dynasty Ceramics", in *Chinese Ceramics: From the Palaeolithic Period through the Qing Dynasty*, edited by Li Zhiyan, Virginia L. Bower, and He Li (New Haven: Yale University Press, 2010), p. 332.

3. Ibid., p. 375.

4. Li Baoping and Weng Yanjun, *New Finds of Yuan Dynasty Blue-and-White Porcelain from the Luomaqiao Kiln Site, Jingdezhen: An Archaeological Approach* (London: Unicorn, 2021).

5. Li Dejin, Jiang Zhongyi, and Guan Jiakun, "Chinese Porcelain Found in a Shipwreck on the Seabed off Sinan, Korea", *The Southeast Asian Ceramic Society: Chinese Translations no. 2* (Singapore: Southeast Asian Ceramic Society, 1980), pp. 25–50.

6. Michael Flecker, "The Jade Dragon Wreck: Sabah, East Malaysia", *Mariner's Mirror* 98, no. 1 (2012): 9–29.

7. Sten Sjostrand and Claire Barnes, "The *Turiang*: A Fourteenth-Century Chinese Shipwreck, Upsetting Southeast Asian Ceramic History", *Journal of the Malaysian Branch of the Royal Asiatic Society* 74, no. 1 (2001): 71–109.

8. Roxanne M. Brown, *The Ming Gap and Shipwreck Ceramics in Southeast Asia: Towards a Chronology of Thai Trade Ware* (Bangkok: Siam Society, 2009), p. 39.

9. "The Yuan Dynasty Shipwreck Site of Dalian Island", *Chinese Archaeology*, China (2014).

10. "Survey Report of the Shiyu Wreck Site in the Paracel Islands", *Journal of the National Museum of China* (2011): 26–46.

11. Li Guoqing, "Archaeological Evidence for the Use of 'Chu-nam' on the 13th Century Quanzhou Ship, Fujian Province, China", *International Journal of Nautical Archaeology* 18, no. 4 (1989): 277–83.

12. Roxanne M. Brown, *The Ming Gap and Shipwreck Ceramics in Southeast Asia: Towards a Chronology of Thai Trade Ware* (Bangkok: Siam Society, 2009), p. 39.

13. Sayan Prishanchit, "Maritime Trade from the Fourteenth to the Seventeenth Century: Evidence from the Underwater Archaeological Sites in the Gulf of Siam", in *The Silk Roads: Highways of Culture and Commerce*, edited by Vadime Elisseeff (New York: Berghahn Books, 2000), p. 190.

14. Jeremy N. Green, "Nautical Archaeology in Australia, the Indian Ocean, and Asia", in *Maritime Archaeology: Australian Approaches* (New York: Springer, 2006), p. 106.

15. Michael Flecker, "The Bakau Wreck: An Early Example of Chinese Shipping in Southeast Asia", *International Journal of Nautical Archaeology* 30, no. 2 (2001): 221–30.

16. Roxanne M. Brown, *The Ming Gap and Shipwreck Ceramics in Southeast Asia: Towards a Chronology of Thai Trade Ware* (Bangkok: Siam Society, 2009), p. 172.

38   Michael Flecker

17. Prishanchit, "Maritime Trade", p. 190.

18. Brown, *The Ming Gap*, p. 173.

19. Roxanne M. Brown and Sten Sjostrand, *Maritime Archaeology and Shipwreck Ceramics in Malaysia* (Kuala Lumpur: Department of Museums and Antiquities, 2002).

3

The International History of Temasek: Possibilities for Research Emerging from the Discovery of the Temasek Wreck

Derek Heng

The state of scholarship on the pre-modern history of Singapore is rich. There has been a significant amount of research conducted, in particular, on the fourteenth century, or the Temasek period. These include almost four decades of archaeological excavations as well as a much longer tradition of textual analyses.

The discovery of the Temasek Wreck, a mid-fourteenth-century vessel that appears to have been on its way from South China to Southeast Asia when it foundered off what would eventually become the territorial waters of present-day Singapore, and which was possibly on its way to Temasek, appears at first glance to be a continuation of the research trajectory we are presently on. However, unlike the land-based excavation sites that continue to be opened, the discovery of this wreck, the first of its kind in Singapore waters, and in many ways the first of its kind in Southeast Asia, has the potential to expand our understanding of Singapore's pre-modern history in areas that scholars have hitherto not been able to embark upon.

This essay seeks to discuss the possibilities of new areas of research into the international history of Temasek, a late-thirteenth to early fifteenth-century port-polity centred on the north bank of the Singapore River. Specifically, it will explore the gaps in our current understanding of Temasek's international economy, its functions as a commercial port at the southern end of the Melaka Strait, its place in the larger Southeast Asian and Maritime East Asian world, and how data from the Temasek Wreck could potentially help to unlock these areas of research.

The State of Scholarship on the Pre-modern International History of Temasek

Presently, historians have narrated Temasek as likely to have functioned as an international entrepôt serving as a trans-shipment hub for products coming from Southeast Asia, the Bay of Bengal littoral and South China Sea littoral. Historical texts and archaeological research indicate that a wide range of trade products, including Chinese ironware, ceramics and silks, flora material such as cotton, fauna products such as hornbill casques, and minerals such as tin and gold, were made available at Banzu—the main port of Temasek. This international economy was complemented by cultural traits maintained by the people of Temasek, including the presence and possible usage of Chinese and Javanese coinage, the adoption of Old Javanese in epigraphic writing, and the import of Javanese religious items for local use, including the importation of lead figurines of the Hindu deity Surya mounted on a winged horse.

Nonetheless, the nature of our knowledge of the Temasek period is centred primarily on the domestic and internal, or endogenous, experiences of the inhabitants of the settlement on the north bank of the Singapore River, and the members of the polity that were located there.[1] These include a fairly comprehensive understanding of the ceramics consumption patterns of the population, the demographic distribution of the settlement based on the differentiated distribution of material cultural remains recovered through archaeology, some of the metallurgical activities conducted along the shores of the Singapore River, including copper and iron working, the rituals related to the rulers of Temasek, and the culinary practices of the inhabitants, including the production of rice wine.[2] There are, in fact, significant gaps in our knowledge of this important period of history. Chief amongst these is the international history of Temasek. What was the nature of Temasek's diplomatic relations with the rest of the world? What was the non-indigenous or non-local demographic of the settlement? What was the nature of Temasek's external economy? These are important questions, as we often identify Temasek with the modern and contemporary port-city of Singapore. While the artefacts recovered from Temasek-period sites point towards the possibility that the population was favourably disposed towards external sources of consumer products, the role and the extent that the external economy played in shaping the society of Temasek is not always evident.

So, what do we know about Temasek's international economic history at present? We know that the regional system of trade that Temasek operated in was the outcome of the trade policies of tier-one states in Maritime Asia, particularly China. With the Middle Eastern states in a period of recession at this time because of the collapse of the Abbasid Dynasty in 1258, coupled with the decline of the maritime-oriented South Indian kingdoms of Chola and Pandya in the late thirteenth and fourteenth centuries, China was able to wield a significant influence over Southeast Asia's commercial environment.[3] With its massive manufacturing capacity and high levels of material technologies, large quantities of high-fired ceramics were imported by Southeast Asian port-cities, including Temasek. The range and volume of Chinese storage jar sherds recovered at Temasek and many other Southeast Asian port-settlement sites also indicate that the region maintained a consistent import trade of Chinese foodstuffs during this time.[4] This information has enabled scholars to map Temasek's consumption patterns between China's economic hinterlands along the south coastal provinces of Guangzhou, Fujian and Zhejiang, which appear to have been consistently maintained through the late thirteenth and fourteenth centuries.

What is still not well understood, however, is the volume and intensity of the economic exchanges between Temasek and China, even though it is clear that Chinese consumer products such as ironware, ceramics, foodstuffs and textiles were imported by Temasek in fairly large volumes. What, for example, was the typical composition of Chinese trade goods that were shipped to Temasek on a typical merchant vessel leaving China for Southeast Asia during this time? What was the qualitative and quantitative nature of Temasek's redistributive and trans-shipment trade of Chinese goods (i.e., what types of products were trans-shipped or redistributed through Singapore, and at what proportions of the incoming cargo)? These important questions can only be answered through the availability of information outside of the Temasek settlement-sites that could be co-related to existing land-archaeology data.

The discovery and excavation of the Temasek Wreck—tentatively dated to the mid-fourteenth century—is important because it represents the first pre-modern shipwreck excavated within Singapore's territorial waters that can be associated with the activities of Temasek. Carrying a cargo composed predominantly of celadon ware, as well as a smaller but nonetheless important cache of blue-and-white porcelain and whiteware,[5] how might the Temasek Wreck be the key to help scholars broach the hitherto unanswered questions pertaining to Temasek's international economy?

Temasek's Commercial Relations with China

A missing piece of information in our studies of Temasek has been the typical quantity of products brought by a vessel from China to Temasek during the fourteenth century. Such information on the broader Southeast Asian trade has been provided through the excavation of shipwrecks in the region's waters. For Singapore, while the corpus of data on shipwrecks in Southeast Asia does exist for the late thirteenth and fourteenth centuries, these have thus far been confined to the Jade Dragon (possibly early fourteenth century), Turiang (late fourteenth to early fifteenth century) and Binh Chau (late fourteenth century) wrecks.[6] Of these, only the Turiang is at a relatively close geographical proximity to Temasek. The Jade Dragon Wreck may be associated with the port-city of Brunei and the eastern route from South China that traversed the Philippines, Sulu zone and the north coast of Borneo Island. The Binh Chau Wreck would have been reflective of the Vietnam coastal trade with China. In other words, the Temasek Wreck potentially serves as the sole source of information on shipping and trade from South China to the immediate area around Temasek, but also the only source of shipping information for Southeast Asia's international trade during the mid-fourteenth century.

The nature of the cargo of a wreck provides indications as to whether the wreck represents a high-frequency trade between China and Southeast Asia, or a redistributive trade within Southeast Asia itself. Large quantities of specific types of products—such as ceramics from a relatively small range of kilns, or large quantities of ironware with a limited number of forms—would typically represent a region-to-region trade. Wrecks that exhibit such a characteristic include the Belitung, Cirebon, Pulau Buaya, Nanhai 1 and Quanzhou wrecks. A diverse cargo with relatively small quantities of categories of goods would typically represent intraregional shipping. Wrecks that exhibit such a characteristic include the Intan and Turiang wrecks.[7]

Was Temasek's trade with China a high-frequency, direct trade, or one that relied primarily on the redistributive networks of other entrepôts in Southeast Asia? Preliminary data from the Temasek Wreck suggests that this trade was probably direct. Many of the blue-and-white porcelain sherds recovered from the wreck site bear decorative motifs similar to those recovered from the Temasek habitation sites, particularly those excavated from Fort Canning Hill. This suggests that the consumption preferences of the inhabitants of the hill, likely the sociopolitical elite of

Temasek, were met by the ceramic production market in South China. This direct link may also be extended to the Longquan celadon recovered from both the Temasek habitation sites and the wreck. Presently, databases on the ceramics recovered from Temasek's habitation sites, including their decorative motifs, are being created. As the data on the ceramics from the Temasek Wreck is established, the above proposition can be tested more effectively.

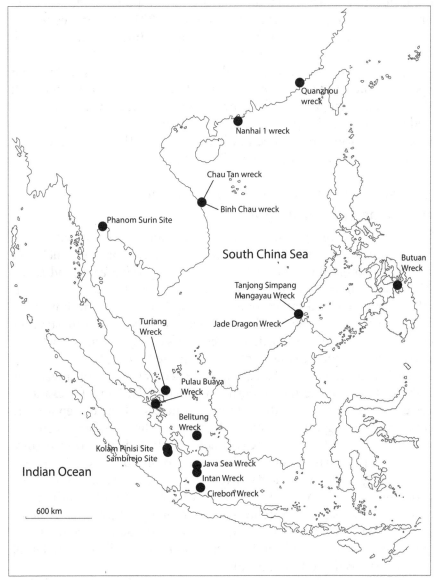

Figure 3.1 Map of shipwrecks in Southeast Asia and South China (ninth through fifteenth centuries).

A closely related question to the above would be: What was the typical composition of trade goods exported from China to Temasek? Herein, wrecks are critically important as they are a time capsule and provide a snapshot of the nature of trade at a particular time. With the Temasek Wreck preliminarily dated to between the 1350s and 1370s, how would the data on this shipment of goods to Temasek correlate with what we already know of Chinese maritime trade policies under the Yuan Dynasty? Yuan maritime trade, through the course of the late thirteenth to fourteenth century, had undergone significant policy shifts—initially under the monopoly of the Ortaq clique (1281–85), proceeded by competition between the clique and the Yuan administration (1285–97). This was followed by an inconsistent oscillation between state monopoly and private trade being permitted (1297–1323), to eventually being operated fully under private concerns (1323–68).[8] With the Temasek Wreck tentatively falling under the last policy period, when maritime trade was fully under private operations, how would the wreck's cargo reflect the relationship between China's policy and the actual practice of export trade to a port-city such as Temasek?

Temasek's Import, Trans-shipment Trade and Domestic Consumption

The current historiography of Temasek positions the port-city as an international entrepôt of the southern Melaka Strait region. This conclusion has been supported by information from the *Sejarah Melayu* and *Daoyi Zhilue*, as well as from the archaeological materials recovered, which reflect a regional and international corpus.[9] Nonetheless, an important question has thus far remained unresolved: Is it possible to reconstruct or deduce a sense of the proportion of Temasek's entrepôt trade activities in relation to its domestic consumption of imported products?

Such a question has, in fact, been addressed by scholars of Singapore's entrepôt trade during the modern era. Chiang Hai Ding, for example, has conducted a study of the volume and nature of the entrepôt trade conducted through the Straits Settlements in the nineteenth century, with Singapore as the primary case study.[10] Such studies typically require two sets of information, such as the volume of import of specific goods or types of goods on the one hand, and the volume of export of the same goods or types of goods on the other. Chiang was able to utilize the customs manifests that were available through the Straits Settlements archives to reconstruct both the qualitative and quantitative nature of Singapore's entrepôt trade and, by extension, the local consumption of the international goods in question.

In the case of Temasek, in the absence of similar records, scholars would have to rely on archaeological data in order to elucidate such conclusions. The artefacts recovered from Temasek's habitation sites provide us with a sense of the proportions of the different types of imported ceramics that were retained for domestic consumption by the port-city's population. This information may in fact be broken down, on a locational basis, to the various sub-areas of the north bank of the Singapore River and Fort Canning Hill as well. The Temasek Wreck artefacts, on the other hand, would likely provide us with a second set of information, this time from outside of the settlement, which, when classified and quantified along the same framework already applied to materials from the Temasek habitation sites, would allow for comparisons of the proportions of ceramic imports versus the proportions that were obtained for Temasek's consumption. By extension, the proportion that would have been re-exported or trans-shipped could also be ascertained.

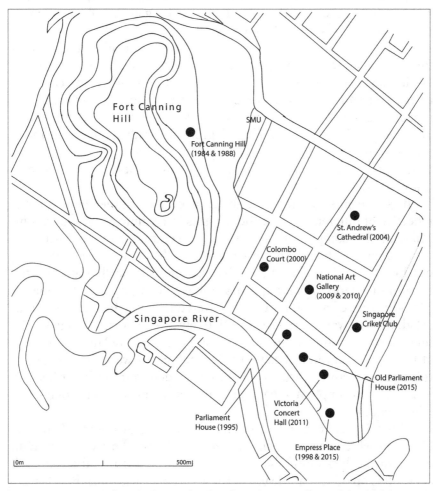

Figure 3.2 Location of Temasek period archaeological sites on the north bank of the Singapore River and Fort Canning Hill.

As an example, we presently know, from post-excavation analyses, that blue-and-white porcelain sherds constitute 12 per cent, 5 per cent, 2 per cent and less than 1 per cent of all fine ceramic sherds recovered from the archaeological sites at Fort Canning Hill, St. Andrew's Cathedral, Old Parliament House and Empress Place, respectively.[11] The preliminary report on the Temasek Wreck by Michael Flecker indicates that blue-and-white porcelain sherds amounted to one hundred and twenty kilograms, or 3 per cent of the total quantity, of ceramic sherds recovered from the wreck site. In comparing the proportions recovered from the land settlement sites and the wreck, it would, at least in the first instance, appear that both the Temasek inhabitants residing at the Fort Canning Hill and St. Andrew's Cathedral sites were retaining proportionally more blue-and-white porcelain for their own usage than that which was brought into Temasek's port by trading vessels. The reverse could be said of the inhabitants residing at the Old Parliament House and Empress Place (1988) sites.

At this preliminary juncture, one can only speculate the reasons for this consumer behaviour. It is possible that the higher unit value of blue-and-white porcelain compared with such other fine ceramics as celadon and whiteware[12] made the former more accessible to the inhabitants of the Fort Canning Hill and St. Andrew's Cathedral sites. The sociopolitical elite were, after all, probably resident on the hill and at the palace precinct, while those closely tied to the sociopolitical elite may have been resident nearby at the foot of the hill where the St. Andrew's Cathedral site is located.

It is also possible that the difference in consumer behaviour is reflective of differences in aesthetic tastes in ceramic decorations. John Miksic, in his comparative analysis of the ceramics recovered from the Fort Canning Hill and Empress Place sites, has noted that in the case of Chinese celadon ware the double-fish motif typically found on the bottom of celadon dishes appears to have been popular at the latter site, while none have so far been recovered from the former site.[13] That celadon ware was consumed in relatively similar proportions by the inhabitants of both sites (62 per cent at Fort Canning Hill; 65 per cent at Empress Place) indicates that price and access was not an issue for this type of ceramic. Taste may have been a determining factor instead. A similar consumption behaviour may have been at play for blue-and-white ceramics.

Third, it has been noted by Lim Tze Siang that the motifs on the blue-and-white porcelain sherds recovered from Fort Canning Hill, including the duck motifs, have not been recovered at any other Temasek sites.[14] It is possible that the use of these ceramics with such motifs were the purview of the sociopolitical elite of Temasek, and therefore not

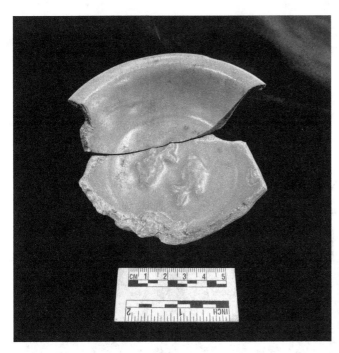

Figure 3.3
Fourteenth-century
Longquan celadon
dish with a double-
fish motif in relief.
(ISEAS)

permitted for use by other groups of the Temasek body politic. Status and exclusivity may have been a factor in determining consumer behaviour.

Conclusion

This essay has sought to open a discussion on the possibilities of historical research following the discovery and excavation of the Temasek Wreck. Hitherto, our knowledge and understanding of Temasek has been based on the bodies of information on the pre-modern port-polity, all of which are confined to the internal characteristics of the Temasek society. The Temasek Wreck presents, for the first time, the opportunity to develop a new body of information that is externally centred, with the possibility of enabling scholars to begin to explore the international history of Temasek from the vantage point of the sea.

While decades of research have provided us with a wealth of information about Temasek's consumption patterns, social hierarchical behaviours and aesthetic tastes, relatively little is known of the dynamics between its import activities, domestic consumption and re-export trade, especially during the time of relative political and economic instability in Yuan China. Expansion of knowledge in this area would enable scholars to better place Singapore's pre-modern history in the broader context of historical developments both in Southeast Asia as well as the larger Maritime Asian world.

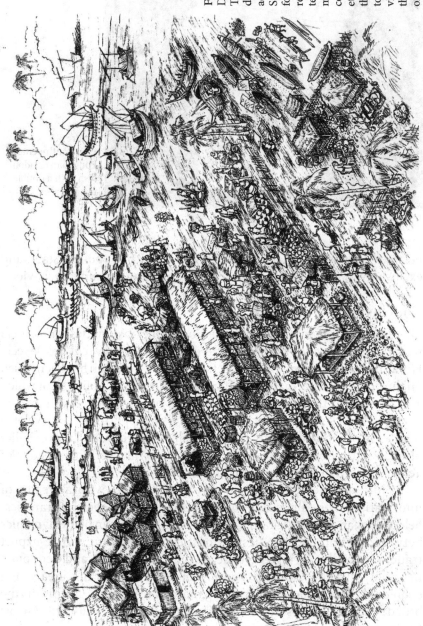

Figure 3.4
Drawing by Aaron Kao. This artist's impression depicts a variety of activities along the Singapore River circa fourteenth century. By referencing ancient text descriptions, early modern illustrations, colonial photographs and ethnographical inferences, this image is an attempt to provide a plausible visualization of events that animated the shores of ancient Singapore.

Finally, the discovery of the Temasek Wreck is a testament to the dynamism of Singapore history as a scholarly field. Just as the discovery of previously unknown archival materials, represented by the work of Peter Borschberg, has greatly illuminated the richness of Singapore's history before 1819, so too the discovery of new sources of information, including shipwrecks, will have a similar impact on our study of Singapore's pre-modern history.

Notes

1. Kwa Chong Guan, Derek Heng, Peter Borschberg, and Tan Tai Yong, *Seven Hundred Years: A History of Singapore* (Singapore: National Library Board and Marshall Cavendish, 2019), pp. 19–49.

2. Derek Heng, "State-Formation and Socio-political Structure of the Malay Coastal Region in the Late Thirteenth to Early Fifteenth Centuries", in *Cross-Cultural Networking in the Eastern Indian Ocean Realm, c.100–1800*, edited by Kenneth R. Hall, Suchandra Ghosh, Kaushik Gangopadhyay, and Rila Mukherjee (Delhi: Primus Books, 2019), pp. 195–220; Shah Alam Zaini, "Metal Production and Social Organisation in Fourteenth-Century Singapore", *Journal of Southeast Asian Studies* 50, no. 4 (2019): 489–506; Derek Heng, "Regional Influences, Economic Adaptation and Cultural Articulation: Diversity and Cosmopolitanism in Fourteenth Century Singapore", *Journal of Southeast Asian Studies* 50, no. 4 (2019): 476–88; Andrea Acri, "Tracing Transregional Networks and Connections across the Indic Manuscript Cultures of Nusantara (AD 1400–1600)", in *Records, Recoveries, Remnants and Inter-Asian Interconnections: Decoding Cultural Heritage*, edited by Anjana Sharma (ISEAS – Yusof Ishak Institute, 2018), pp. 184–221.

3. Kwa et al., *Seven Hundred Years*, pp. 21–25.

4. Derek Heng, "Economic Exchanges and Linkages between the Malay Region and the Hinterland of Quanzhou and Guangzhou: Temasek and the Chinese Ceramics and Foodstuffs Trade", in *Early Singapore, 1300s–1819: Evidence in Maps, Text and Artefacts,* edited by Cheryl-Ann Low Mei Gek and John N. Miksic (Singapore: Singapore History Museum, 2004), pp. 73–85.

5. Michael Flecker, *The Temasek Wreck (mid-14th Century), Singapore – Preliminary Report*, Temasek Working Paper Series no. 4 (Singapore: ISEAS – Yusof Ishak Institute, 2022), pp. 1–82.

6. Michael Flecker, "The Jade Dragon Wreck: Sabah, East Malaysia", *Mariner's Mirror* 98, no. 1 (2012): 9–29; Sten Sjøstrand and Claire Barnes, "The *Turiang*: a Fourteenth-Century Chinese Shipwreck Upsetting Southeast Asian Ceramic History", *Journal of the Malaysian Branch of the Royal Asiatic Society* 74, no. 1 (2001): 71–109; Flecker, *The Temasek Wreck*, pp. 56–57.

7. Derek Heng, "Ships, Shipwrecks and Archaeological Recoveries as Sources of Southeast Asian History", in *Oxford Research Encyclopedia of Asian*

History, edited by David Ludden (New York: Oxford University Press, 2018), https://doi.org/ 10.1093/acrefore/9780190277727.013.97.

8. Herbert Franz Schurmann, *Economic Structure of the Yüan Dynasty* (Cambridge, MA: Harvard University Press, 1967); Derek Heng, *Sino Malay Trade and Diplomacy from the Tenth through the Fourteenth Century* (Athens: Ohio University Press, 2009), pp. 63–71.

9. *Sejarah Melayu or Malay Annals,* translated by C.C. Brown (Kuala Lumpur: Oxford University Press, 1970); Su Jiqing, *Daoyi zhilue xiaoju* [Treatise on the island barbarians] (Bejing: Zhonghua shuju, 1991).

10. Chiang Hai Ding, *A History of Straits' Settlements Foreign Trade, 1870–1915* (Singapore: National Museum, 1978).

11. John N. Miksic, "Beyond the Grave: Excavations North of the Kramat Iskandar Shah, 1988", *Heritage* 10 (1989): 34–56.

12. Lim Tse Siang, "14th Century Singapore: The Temasek Paradigm" (MA Thesis, Department of History, National University of Singapore, 2012), pp. 106–7.

13. John N. Miksic, "Recently Discovered Chinese Green Glazed Wares of the Thirteenth and Fourteenth Centuries in Singapore and the Riau Islands", in *New Light on Chinese Yue and Longquan Wares,* edited by Ho Chuimei (Hong Kong: University of Hong Kong, 1994); Lim, "14th Century Singapore", p. 109; Heng, *Sino-Malay Trade,* p. 223.

14. Lim, "14th Century Singapore", pp. 165–66.

4

Singapore's Waterways before the Modern Era

Benjamin J.Q. Khoo

Standing at the beach in East Coast Park, the eye is struck immediately by the huge ocean liners and cargo ships anchored out at sea as far as the horizon. On an exceptionally clear day it is possible to see as far as Batam, just across the Singapore Strait. At night, the lights from the ships come on, like shimmering little bonfires dotting the line of water. From land, this is an image of idyllic calm and irrepressible peace, with the sound of the waves taking one far from the chaos and bustle of the city. Yet this image is deceptive. Unless one has spent time at sea, it would not be immediately apparent that the reality is far less irenic and immutable. Indeed, for much of Singapore's history, the waters in and around the island had an unsavoury reputation as a place of danger and death. Traversing the Singapore Straits in the past often tested the mettle of a captain, and recounting this experience of the voyage formed a favourite subject in tales and lore, many of which have been forgotten today. The aim of this essay therefore is to provide a short history of sailing past Singapore, to familiarize those on terra firma with the four different waterways that sailors used and the incipient dangers they faced when navigating past the island before

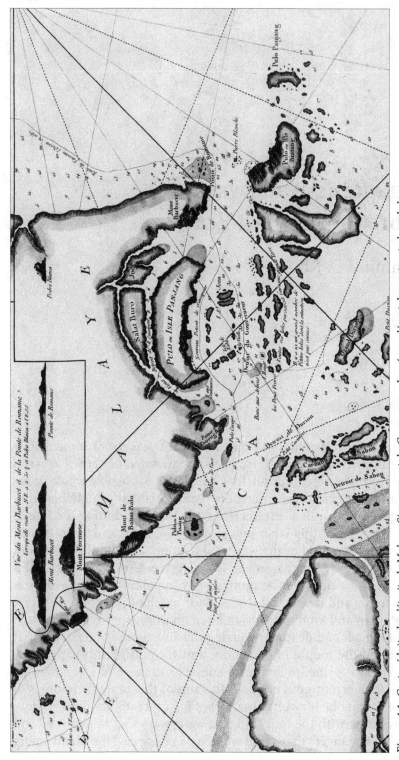

Figure 4.1 *Carte réduite des détroits de Malaca, Sincapour, et du Gouverneur dressée au dépost des cartes et plans de la marine.* Jacques Nicolas Bellin, 1755. Collection of National Library, Singapore. Accession no.: B18153062D.

the modern era. This brief overview will equip the reader with a more seaward perspective and help to locate Singapore's arteries within a larger maritime framework.[1]

Defining the Singapore Straits

The Singapore Strait (singular) is a body of water situated south of the Island of Singapore, separating the tip of the Malay Peninsula from the islands of Riau. Running approximately 113 kilometres in length, it includes small islands and reefs and merges, from west to east, the Melaka Strait and the Karimata Strait with the South China Sea. Today, the narrowest navigable part of the strait is between Singapore's southernmost island, Pulau Satumu, and Indonesia's Pulau Takong Besar, which is a distance of a mere 5.2 kilometres. Its widest point, by contrast, measures some 20 kilometres, between Malaysia's Tanjong Rumania and Bintan, of Indonesia's Riau Islands archipelago. Because regional and long-distance trading networks converge at this narrow and congested corridor, it has long been celebrated as an important meeting point for goods, people and ideas. But its prominence has also aroused the envy of empires, who sought to control this strategic funnel and project their power throughout history.

In the Age of Sail, successfully navigating past Singapore depended on the monsoon winds. From November to March, the northeast monsoon prevails, whilst from June through to September, the wind direction changes course, blowing from the southwest. During the inter-monsoon months, wind flow is light and variable. Not too long ago, junks from China, Vietnam and Thailand would come with the northeast monsoon to this part of the world and leave with the seasonal change. Local and regional vessels coming from Sumatra and Java, on the other hand, usually took the southwest monsoon and left before the onset of the northeast.[2] The monsoon winds affect the surface currents and can exacerbate the sea swells. Furthermore, interactions between tide-induced and monsoonal waves add further complexity and irregularity to its waters. Other dangers here concern the climatic conditions and maritime raiding. Mainly between March and November, lines of thunderstorm form over Sumatra and sweep eastward towards Singapore, hitting often at early dawn. These sudden gusts of wind and heavy rain are called Sumatran squalls and, although they last no longer than an hour or two, are enough to take ships and their crew by surprise.[3] These squalls might have explained early Portuguese references to Singapore as *falsa demora* or a "wrong or tricky place to stay".[4] Besides the unexpected weather, the multitude of islands—complete with dense vegetation, narrow inlets, bays and creeks—also presented a host of risks for the passing ship since they formed ideal hideouts for pirates for ambush and plunder, which indeed found widespread practice in the vicinity and proved a subject of constant complaint.

The Singapore Straits (plural) is a collective term commonly applied to several maritime routes in and around these waters. Before the modern era, a sailor was able to choose from four different waterways. The first is the Old Strait; second, the New Strait; third, the Tebrau Strait (known today as the Strait of Johor); and finally, the Governor's Strait. These maritime passages were continually traversed by vessels, although, as we shall see, some gradually passed out of employment by preference and fell out of notice in consequence.

A Short Early History of Sailing past Singapore

It is without question that knowledge of the maritime routes in and around Singapore was part of the inscrutable ancient wisdom of the sea peoples and local pilots from mainland and insular Southeast Asia long before instructions were set down on paper. Historically, the use of the Singapore waterway first become evident with the rise of Srivijaya, a thalassocratic empire on Sumatra that emerged around the seventh century CE. Srivijaya projected its power into the Singapore and Melaka Straits by sending ships to ply these waters and control commodity flows in and around the region.[5]

From the ninth century CE onwards, the value of the Singapore Straits as a direct transoceanic route connecting two large trading circuits—the Indian Ocean and the South China Sea—increased. This is

Figure 4.2 "Batu Berlayer" or "Lot's wife", by J.T. Thomson, 1848. PA-0539-A.

evidenced by references in early Chinese texts and Arab sailing rutters around this period, which suggest a growing cognizance and increased use of this waterway.[6] Commercial expansion during the Yuan period in the twelfth century meant that Chinese ships did undertake several voyages, including one by the Yuan general Yang Tingbi, who likely crossed the Singapore Strait between 1279 and 1282 CE.[7] It is not until the fourteenth century, however, that the first concrete mention of the Singapore Strait as a waterway appears. This reference comes from the oft-cited account of Wang Dayuan—the *Daoyi Zhilüe* (A Brief Account of Island Barbarians, 1349). His description indicated a waterway that was flanked by two hills the shape of dragon's teeth. This geological resemblance is taken to refer to the rocky outcrops that once stood at Batu Berlayar Point, near Labrador Park, which have been credited as a reference to ancient Singapore and its accompanying waterway, the Old Strait.[8]

It is presumably this channel that was used by the Ming fleets of Grand Admiral Zheng He as they fanned out into Southeast Asia, crossing into the Melaka Strait in the early fifteenth century.[9] Even though the Malay records have not directly referenced its use, we are left with no doubt that it was a prominent passage as it was deeply enshrined in memory and lore. Evidence of this can be gleaned from texts such as the *Sejarah Melayu* and the *Hikayat Hang Tuah*, as well as the later Portuguese chronicles that record the consolidated memories of the villages of Melaka. From the fateful and tumultuous crossing of Sang Nila Utama, who abandoned all cargo before he reached Temasek, to the recorded "histories" of Parameswara, who made himself "Lord of the Strait", purportedly set in the late thirteenth century, to the capture of the strait and the island of Bintan by Sultan Muzaffar Shah of Melaka in the fifteenth century, what emerges from these accounts is not only a continued use of the Singapore Straits by local *perahu*[10] and ships, but also as an aquatic space and strategic chokepoint that kingdoms struggled for control over.[11]

In looking at sailing past Singapore in its early history, we can reasonably assume that this referred to the use of the Old Strait (detailed below). The historian Gibson-Hill speculates that no other channel was used by Asian mercantile vessels or smaller native crafts since there was no clear incentive to do so—the fear of venturing into the unknown served as a sufficient deterrent to exploration.[12] The discovery, however, of a fourteenth-century shipwreck on Pulau Nipa (Tree Island) in the 1980s, further west of Pulau Satumu, seems to suggest otherwise. But if earlier sailing notices were ill-defined, this was to change with the arrival of the Europeans, who have left us with copious records of passage as well as their discoveries of alternative routes for sailing past Singapore.

The Four Waterways

(1) The Old Strait

After the Portuguese took Melaka in 1511, they began collecting information about the surrounding lands and waterways, outfitting ships for voyages that took them through the Singapore Straits. Drawing upon the knowledge of local and foreign pilots (notably the Arabs and the Chinese), they were the first Europeans consistently using the route through the Old Strait of Singapore.

In order to take this route, sailing from west to east, the travelling ship makes a sharp turn from the Karimun Islands towards the Sembilan Strait. It then follows along the coast of Singapore, skirting by Pasir Panjang, before arriving at the aforementioned pillar-shaped rock, Batu Berlayar. From this prominent landmark, the sailor would then set a northeastern course, heading for the narrow passage between Sentosa and the mainland. After successfully navigating this channel, the vessel continues by following the eastern coast of Singapore to its next landmark, the stone outcropping of Pedra Branca, before exiting into the South China Sea.

From as early as 1511, the conqueror of Melaka, Alfonso de Albuquerque, had sent a Portuguese named Duarte Fernandes, who passed through the Singapore Straits with letters to Siam. Albuquerque seems to have used the passage himself, sailing to the Gate (*Porta*) of Singapore, where he encountered the Laksamana in the aftermath of Melaka's capture. The use of this passage was set down in writing a few years later; the rutter of Francisco Rodrigues of 1513 records this route in detail and shows how it took ships from Melaka to Canton (Guangdong), passing through the Karimun Islands, Singapore and Pedra Branca.[13] Another early testimony is found in the work of the Portuguese apothecary Tomé Pires, his *Suma Oriental* (1512–15), which also references the Old Strait as a channel with a few villages. Arguably, knowledge of this waterway is best codified in the *Book of Seamanship* (1525) by John of Lisbon, which represented one of the most detailed rutters for making this passage through the Old Strait in the early sixteenth century.

The later use of the Old Strait (also called by the Portuguese the Canal de Varela) is described in great detail by many European sources, which often relate the treachery of making this crossing. Almost every account remarks on how slender the passage was, being not more than a stone's throw in breadth and about the length of a cannon's shot. Beneath the line of water were stones and sandbanks, which were only exposed at low tide. These could scrape the hull of a vessel and cause untold damage to both ship and cargo. Furthermore, the tides here are swift and

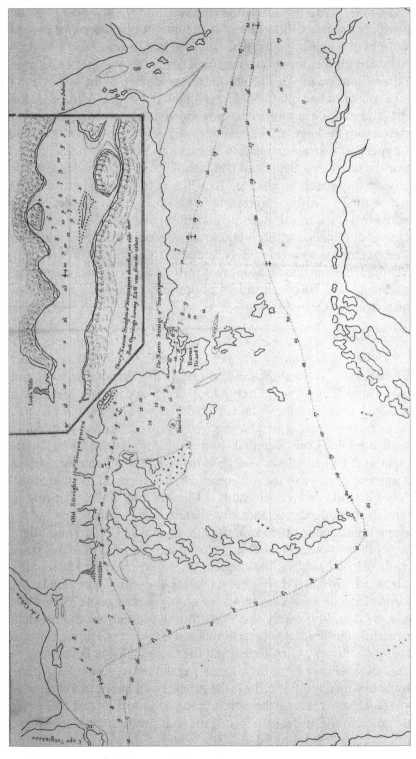

Figure 4.3 "Chart of the Straits of Sinkapoura from an old book of English Mss" © The British Library Board. Shelfmark: 17_X36242135B1003.

unpredictable, sometimes running one way and then suddenly going in the opposite direction. The result is that vessels, when not caught unaware by the shifting currents, were obliged to wait for a few days and take careful measurements before making the crossing, sometimes with the help of smaller boats or with the assistance of the local Orang Laut. Larger ships had other incidental difficulties to deal with. Since the islands around the strait were overgrown with large sprawling trees that interfered with the large-sail vessels cutting through the narrow channel, the skippers on board often had to be cautious that these branches did not tear the sails or break masts during strong currents or winds.[14] While waiting for the current to change, the still and forbidding nature of the landscape made a strong impression, with one writer once describing the scenery as "tedious, lonesome and uninteresting".[15] Furthermore, the cluster of dangers, without taking into account sudden changes of weather or ambush by local raiders, added to the difficulty of traversing this channel. It is for these reasons that the Old Strait earned a fearsome reputation among European sailors as the "most dangerous passage in all the seas of the Orient".[16]

(2) The New Strait

In 1584, the Portuguese in Melaka became embroiled in a conflict with Johor. Portuguese ships sailed down to the Singapore Straits and blockaded the Johor River, forcing local ships to divert to Melaka. In retaliation, Sultan Ali Jalla Abdul Jalil Shah II, who oversaw Johor Lama's rise as a centre of trade, and who was well aware of Portuguese shipping through the Old Strait, decided on a cunning plan. As soon as the Portuguese ships had lifted the siege of his river, the sultan dispatched a large number of ships to the Singapore Straits. There, in the Old Strait, the Johor armada deliberately sank old barges and junks, throwing in logs and driftwood for good measure, thereby clogging up the end of the constricted passage. At the same time, he instructed the roving might of the sea fleet to redirect local ships to Johor. When news of this trade blockade reached Melaka, the Captain of Melaka, João de Silva, sent a squadron, which sailed through the Old Strait of Singapore. Finding it thus impeded, the crew cast about for an alternative route among the islands. By doubling south, the ships found another channel, which, after careful sounding, was determined to be wide enough for ships to pass through. This was first christened the Canal of Santa Barbara.[17]

This channel later came to be known as the New Strait of Singapore, the route of which roughly follows the itinerary set out by its Portuguese discovers. Upon reaching the outcropping of Batu Berlayar, the ships would sail outwards instead, following the southwestern coast of Sentosa, passing north of St. John's Island. The vessels then sailed through the

Figure 4.4 Discripsao Chorographica dos estreitos de Sincapura e Sabbam Ano 1604, Manuel Godinho de Erédia, from *Malaca, L'Inde Orientale et le Cathay*. (Collection of National Library, Singapore. Accession no.: B03013605G)

Buran channel. After making this crossing, ships have a clear run along the eastern coast of Singapore towards the Johor River estuary before sailing on into the vicinity of Pedra Branca. This new fork in the road is memorably depicted in a draft chart by the Portuguese mestizo Manoel Godinho de Erédia (1604). Although erroneous in scale, both the lines dotting the Old and New Strait of Singapore (*Estreito Velho and Estreito Novo*) are clearly marked, alongside other important features on the island of Singapore.

The dangers of the New Strait of Singapore are similar to those of the Old, with references to current changes and dangerous shoals. Some distinction was made, no doubt, between the two passages by seasoned mariners, and the New Strait was used by several crossings well into the seventeenth century. Evidence of this comes from 1613, when the English ship *The Globe* made use of this strait, taking a local pilot in order to navigate the passage.[18] Passing through the New Strait was not without some advantage. The Flemish gem trader Jacques de Coutre noted in his memorials that the shores along the New Strait of Singapore were better suited for *bantin* and galleys to land and bring in supplies.[19] Despite this discovery, however, it seems the New Strait was little frequented. As a waterway, it continued to be remembered well into the late eighteenth century, and it remained a viable option. But the Old Strait seemed to be the preferred choice, especially until the end of the seventeenth century, being of greater familiarity and longer antiquity.

(3) The Tebrau Strait

Unlike the Old and New Straits of Singapore, which tend to prevail in the extant literature, the Tebrau Strait, known today as the Johor Strait, is less familiar. This strait extends northward, following the northern coastline of Singapore, taking ships between the Island of Singapore and the mainland of Johor. Ships arriving from the Melaka Strait would keep a lookout for the promontory of Tanjung Bulus at the southernmost tip of Malaysia, where a curve in the water forms a noticeable entrance. Situated less than twenty kilometres from this point, the waterway flows inwards into Johor, or Ujong Tanah as it was known. At the shallowest point, the depth was said to be only three *brazas*.[20] Taking this route meant that vessels would have sailed past Pulau Merembong, hugging the northern coast of Singapore, before reaching Pulau Ubin. This islet splits the water into two channels, and the journey through this waterway ends by taking a more southerly route, sailing towards the Johor River estuary, where ships found themselves in more familiar waters.

It has yet to be historically evidenced when this waterway was discovered. The *Reysgheschrift* (1595) of Jan Huygen van Linschoten, for example, ascribes its accidental use by a certain Antonio de

Melo, who sailed through the waterway with a ship of eight hundred *bahars*, [21]thereafter emerging at the Johor River estuary. However, van Linschoten gives no dates nor credits de Melo with this discovery.[22] Perceptive readers would also have spotted Salat Tubro (Selat Tebrau or Tebrau Strait) marked on Erédia's chart of 1604, pointing to an earlier cognizance and possible use of the waterway. This charting here also indicates that the Tebrau Strait appeared to the Portuguese as an estuary of the Johor River.[23] The Dutch academic Gerret Pieter

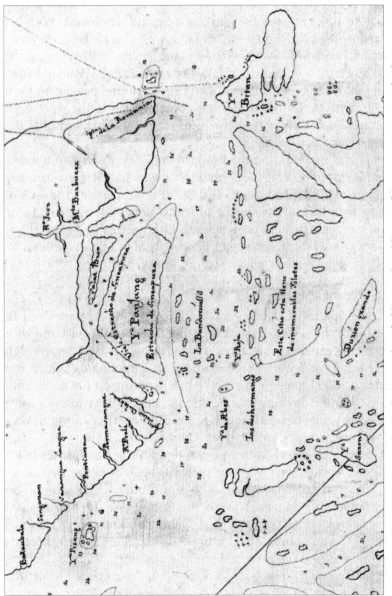

Figure 4.5 The Tebrau Strait with soundings, misidentified here as the Old Strait of Singapore (*Viejo Estrecho de Sincapura*), Carta plan segunda parte del Estrecho de Malaca desde las Yslas de Daru hasta la de Pulotimon, etc. Library of Congress Geography and Map Division Washington, D.C. G9182.M2 17-- .C3.

Rouffaer suggests that Dutch vessels did make use of the passage when they arrived at the beginning of the seventeenth century.[24] An important testimony corroborating this view concerns the ship the *Griffioen*, which camped out close to Pulau Ubin in the Tebrau Strait in 1609 on the lookout for Portuguese ships trying to blockade the Johor River.[25] Besides these textual clues, maps produced after the 1660s also show a distinct knowledge of the islands in the Johor Strait, which indicates an awareness of the Tebrau passage. As one of the later writings of note, in 1816, Sir Stamford Raffles published a short piece for the Asiatic Society in Bengal. This article included a story about a Minangkabau prince who sailed to Johor to seek the hand of a beautiful princess. With his retinue and *perahu*, the prince was said to have sailed to the entrance of the Tebrau Strait, where he was checked and repelled.[26] This lone story, undated in origin, was said to explain the existence of a Minangkabau village in Johor, and perhaps point to an earlier use and passage by local vessels. But with the shift of the Johor court to Riau in the eighteenth century, there was little reason for Europeans to sail up towards the Johor estuary and mainland.

In texts and maps before the modern era, it is possible to observe some confusion concerning the Tebrau Strait, which is often erroneously described or misidentified as the Old Strait of Singapore. The lack of familiarity with this strait and the absence of notable shipwrecks or records of incidents perhaps suggest it was little used by European ships. The waterway was most certainly plied by local craft and avoided by larger, ocean-going vessels, which steered further south.

(4) The Governor's Strait

In 1616, the Spanish Governor of Manila, Juan de Silva, arrived in Singapore with the largest armada ever assembled in the East and with the intention of expelling the Dutch in one fell swoop. With hubris high and strategy secondary, the mission ended in ignominious failure, but not before de Silva made a discovery that would etch his name into water. This was the opening of a new route, named after Juan de Silva and his fleet that first passed through there: the Governor's Strait.[27] After joining with two ships coming from China, Juan de Silva decided to sail through a "new strait" (*estreito novo*) that was located further south of Singapore. This journey was not without incident as the governor's 2000-ton flagship galleon, *La Salvadora*, unfortunately ran aground on a reef. However, the damage was not significant and the journey was otherwise completed successfully, thus opening up a new route for ships to traverse.[28] From its humble beginnings, this channel gradually became the main fairway and the preferred passage of sailors. This is evidenced by the Spanish friar Domingo de Navarette, who commented sometime in the 1670s that the Old Strait of Singapore was falling into gradual disuse in favour of the Governor's Strait, a process that continued well into the eighteenth century.

The clearest description of this route is provided by the French hydrographer Jean-Baptiste d'Après de Mannevillette (1745). Upon sighting the Karimun islands, ships kept a lookout for Pulau Kukup and Tanjung Bulus, off the western Malay Peninsula. After passing Kukup, vessels would head for the easily sighted Pulau Nipa, which marks the entrance of the main waterway. Lining up from Pulau Nipa is a series of islands known today as Singapore's southern islands. The vessel would then carefully wind its way towards the southern end of Pulau Senang, passing between this island and Pulau Biola. After leaving the two islands in its wake, the ship would then set its course towards St. John's Island, making its way towards Tanjung Rumania and then Pedra Branca, or head south towards Batam or Bintan, where Riau had a thriving port. The voyage from China was made through this strait in reverse.

By and large, the Governor's Strait was easier to navigate, though it was not without its inherent dangers. Pilots were warned to stick to a middling course, avoiding the islands south and north, since the various islets also had several dangerous shoals. On the eastern side, there were several sandbanks extending from Singapore. The currents here were said to be strong; the waters were reasonably deep and a seaman needed to pay attention to the direction of the currents. A lack of wind or an opposing current could occasionally mean that a vessel had to anchor

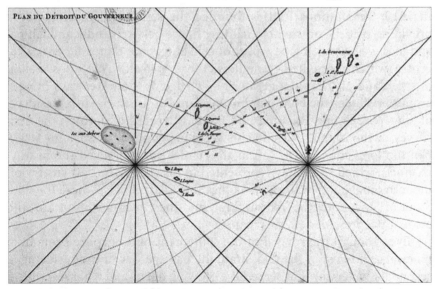

Figure 4.6 Close-up of the Governor's Strait and the islands, viz. from Pulau Nipa (*Ile aux Arbres*) to St. John's Island (*Ile St. Jean*), Gallica, Bibliothèque Nationale de France.

near St. John's Island, a location with several dangerous rocks in the vicinity. Nevertheless, the Governor's Strait was a good choice since the strong currents, when favourable, shortened the voyage considerably. A more attractive consideration was that not only was it less dangerous than the Old and New Straits, but the relatively more open waters also meant it offered greater room to manoeuvre. It is in this strait that in the eighteenth century the Dutch would regularly post patrol ships, which would wait at the western end near Pulau Nipa where they had a good view of the local and international traffic heading down from the Melaka Strait and up from the Durian Strait. These cruisers could also sail through the Governor's Strait towards Pedra Branca, where they could escort important ships coming from the East. The increased use of the Governor's Strait meant fewer encounters with the Orang Laut, and this led to a gradual decline in accounts of Singapore Island in the eighteenth century.

By the early nineteenth century, the Governor's Strait had become so well utilized that it was mistakenly referred to as the "New" Strait of Singapore to distinguish it from the two former channels, which were now rarely used. British ships sailing through this strait in the first years of the 1800s seem to have forgotten much of its dangers. On a gorgeous, plain-sailing day, one writer claimed that "there can scarcely be a more beautiful picture than the sight of a fleet of ships winding through this romantic group of islands".[29]

Conclusion: The Arrival of Steam

In 1819, Sir Stanford Raffles founded the settlement of Singapore, providing British ships with a halfway house between India and China and local vessels with a new port of call. Singapore thereafter rose as a centre, which reoriented trade flows towards itself.[30] With possession of the island also came a greater knowledge of the waterways in and around it. Under the command of William Farquhar, the first Resident of Singapore, James Franklin and Francis Bernard undertook the first survey of the island, as well as its accompanying waterways, in 1822. Not too long after, in 1827, Captain Daniel Ross surveyed the nearby channels, which were duly represented in his chart. The bathymetry of modern Singapore's waterways comes into sharp focus, where the Old Strait of Singapore, the Tebrau Strait and the Governor Strait are still evidently represented on this map.

Even though the revival of the settlement of Singapore brought a renewal of interest in the Old Strait, the passage was only considered a secondary waterway that served the growing docks and wharves, which came to be fondly termed New Harbour. In 1837, the Governor's Strait seems to have been erroneously conflated with the Phillip's Channel,

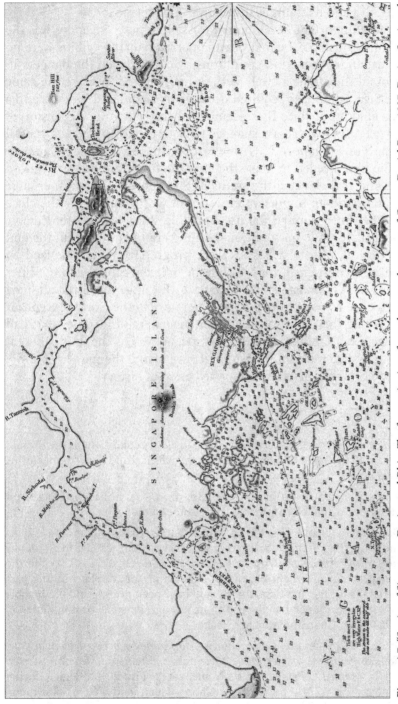

Figure 4.7 "Straits of Singapore, Durian and Rhio. The former is given from the several surveys of Captn. Daniel Ross, 1827. Durian Strait and Phillips Channel by Lieut.s Collinson and Moresby 1822, and Rio Strait by Lieut.s Dittl of Tjassens Royal Dutch Navy 1843, the whole materially corrected by J.T. Thomson Government surveyor at Singapore 1846." © The British Library Board. Shelfmark: SEC.12.(1336).

which links Durian Strait to the Singapore Strait.[31] The result is that very little association is made between the historical exploits of Governor Juan de Silva and its status as the main shipping lane today.

A more important development for sailing past Singapore was the arrival of steamships, the first of which arrived in 1845. Ships were no longer dependent on wind conditions, which reduced the dangers in and around the straits as well as the time required to make the same voyage. Steamships also required deep wharf facilities, dry docks and a copious amount of coal. These demands necessitated the expansion of the port, causing wholesale changes to both the town and the coastal landscape of Singapore.[32] With the opening of the Suez Canal in 1869, the time needed to make the crossing from Europe was reduced further and this elevated the status of Singapore as an indispensable coal station and an important entrepôt in world trade.[33] By the close of the nineteenth century, the use of sailing ships was in irremediable decline. Native trade on traditional sailing craft continued till the end of this period, but these vessels were progressively marginalized by European square-rigged ships.[34] With the influx of capital, commodities and clans rapidly transforming Singapore, the Singapore Strait attained pre-eminence as one of the busiest waterways in the world. Except for those making their living at sea, the dangers and difficulties that had characterized a familiar sailing seascape, as well as the four different routes that once took ships past Singapore before the modern period, were largely forgotten, confined to the basket of history.

Notes

1. I thank Dr Michael Flecker for helping to clarify conditions as they would appear to the sailor and for correcting the nautical and navigational terms used here.

2. South of the equator (for ships arriving from Indonesia) the "southwest monsoon" would be considered the "southeast monsoon".

3. Duy Khiem Ly and Cheng Ann Tan, "Characteristics of Sumatra Squalls and Modelling of the Squall-Generated Waves", *Journées de l'hydraulique: SimHydro 2014. New Trends in Simulation* 36 (2014): 1–12. While the Sumatran squalls might have been frightening for travellers sailing past the straits for the first time, they would have been routine and predictable for seasoned seamen making use of the passage. Personal communication, Kwa Chong Guan and Michael Flecker.

4. Brás de Albuquerque, *Commentarios do Grande Alfonso Dalboquerque, Capitão geral que foi das Indias Orientaes em Tempo do Muito Poderoso Rey D. Manuel O Primeiro deste Nome*, vol. 3 (Lisbon: Na Regia Officina Typografica, 1774), p. 85; Kwa Chong Guan and Peter Borschberg, "Singapore's 'Tricky' Place in Archipelagic History: To Understand Singapore's History, Look At It from the Sea, Not Land", *Straits Times*,

10   October   2018.   https://www.straitstimes.com/opinion/singapores-tricky-place-in-archipelagic-history.

5.   Pierre-Yves Manguin, "Srivijaya: Trade and Connectivity in the Pre-modern Malay World", *Journal of Urban Archaeology* 3 (2021): 91.

6.   Geoff Wade, "Maritime Routes between Indochina and Nusantara to the 18th Century", *Archipel* 85 (2013): 83–104; Tansen Sen, "Maritime Southeast Asia between South Asia and China to the Sixteenth Century", *TRaNS: Trans-Regional and -National Studies of Southeast Asia* 2, no. 1 (2014): 31–59.

7.   Sumio Fukami, "元代のマラッカ海峡　通路か拠点か" [Passage or emporium? The Malacca Strait during the Yuan Period], *Southeast Asia: History and Culture* 33 (2004): 112.

8.   Hsü Yün Ts'iao, "Singapore in the Remote Past", *Journal of the Malaysian Branch of the Royal Asiatic Society (JMBRAS)* 45, no. 1 (1972): 1–9.

9.   Tai Yew Seng, "Zheng He's Navigation Methods and His Visit to Longyamen, Singapore", in *1819 & Before: Singapore's Past*, edited by Kwa Chong Guan (Singapore: ISEAS – Yusof Ishak Institute, 2021), p. 106.

10.   Traditional sailing craft used by Malay and Bugis traders.

11.   C.C Brown, "Sejarah Melayu; or, Malay Annals: A Translation of Raffles MS 18 (In the Library of the RAS, London)", *JMBRAS* 25, nos. 2/3 (1952): 29-30; Armando Cortesão, ed., *The Suma Oriental of Tomé Pires: An Account of the East, from the Red Sea to Japan, Written in Malacca and India in 1512–1515; and, the Book of Francisco Rodrigues, Rutter of a Voyage in the Red Sea, Nautical Rules, Almanack and Maps, Written and Drawn in the East before 1515*, vol. 2 (London: Hakluyt Society, 1944), pp. 232, 244.

12.   C.A. Gibson-Hill, "Singapore Old Strait and New Harbour, 1300–1870", in *Studying Singapore before 1800*, edited by Kwa Chong Guan and Peter Borschberg (Singapore: NUS Press, 2018), p. 232.

13.   Cortesão, *The Suma Oriental*, p. 301.

14.   Francesco Carletti, *My Voyage around the World: The Chronicles of a 16th Century Florentine Merchant* (New York: Pantheon Books, 1964), p. 187.

15.   *A Gazetteer of the World, or Dictionary of Geographical Knowledge, etc.*, vol. 6. (London: Fullarton, 1859), p. 629.

16.   Selvaggio Canturan, *La storia della Chiesa del Giappone del rev. padre Giovanni Crasset* (Venice: Baglioni, 1722), pp. 152–53.

17.   João de Barros and Diogo de Couto, *Da Asia de Diogo de Couto, Dos Feitos, que Os Portuguezes fizeram na Conquista, e Descubrimento das Terras, e Mares do Oriente. Decada Decima, Parte Segunda* (Lisbon: Regia Officina Typografica, 1778), pp. 210–11.

18.   W.H. Moreland, ed., *Peter Floris: His Voyage to the East Indies in the Globe, 1611–1615* (London: Hakluyt Society, 1934), pp. 100–104.

19.   Peter Borschberg, *The Singapore and Melaka Straits: Violence, Security and Diplomacy in the 17th Century* (Singapore: NUS Press, 2010), pp. 120, 246.

20. Manuel Pimentel (1762), *Arte de navegar ... a Roteiro das viagens a costas de Guiné, Angola, Brazil, Indias e Islas occidentaes e orientates* (Lisbon: Officina de Miguel Manescal da Costa, 1762), pp. 422–25. The Portuguese *braza* is approximately 1.76–1.83 metres.

21. *Bahar* is a commonly used unit of weight. The reference here is likely to 800 *bahars* worth of goods. Linschoten ascertains the weight of a *bahar* here to be equivalent to 3.5 Portuguese *quintals* (a common European unit of weight; viz., 128 pounds), which is 448 pounds.

22. Jan Huygen van Linschoten, *Reys-Gheschrift vande Navigatien der Portugaloysers in Orienten, etc.* (Amsterdam: Claesz, 1595), p. 38.

23. Peter Borschberg, "Three Questions about Maritime Singapore, 16th–17th Centuries", *Ler Historia* 72 (2018): 31–54.

24. Gerret Pieter Rouffaer, "Was Malakka Emporium vóór 1400 A.D., Genaamd Malajoer? En waar lag Woerawari Mā-Hasin, Langa, Batoesawar", *Bijdragen tot de Taal-, Land- en Volkenkunde van Nederlandsche-Indië* 77 (1921): 398–99.

25. Borschberg, *The Singapore and Melaka Straits*, pp. 39–40.

26. Thomas Stamford Raffles, "On the Malayu Nation, with a Translation of its Maritime Institutions", *Asiatic Researches; or Transactions of the Society instituted in Bengal, etc.*, vol. 12 (1816): 111.

27. Peter Borschberg, "Security, VOC Penetration and Luso-Spanish Co-operation: The Armada of Philippine Governor Juan de Silva in the Straits of Singapore, 1616", in *Iberians in the Singapore-Melaka Area and Adjacent Regions (16th to 18th Century)*, edited by Peter Borschberg (Wiesbaden: Harrassowitz, 2003), pp. 35–62.

28. António Bocaro, *Decadas 13 da Historia da India, etc. Parte II* (Lisbon: Typographia da Academia Real das Sciencas, 1876), p. 428. See also Gerolamo Emilio Gerini, *Researches on Ptolemy's Geography of Eastern Asia (Further India and Indo-Malay Archipelago)* (London: Royal Asiatic Society, 1909), p. 534n1.

29. James Johnson, *An Account of a Voyage to India, China &c. in His Majesty's Ship Caroline: Performed in the Years 1803-4-5, Interspersed with Descriptive Sketches and Cursory Remarks* (London: Richard Phillips, 1806), pp. 47–48.

30. Howard Dick, Vincent J.H. Houben, J. Thomas Lindblad, and Kian Wie Thee, *Emergence of a National Economy: An Economic History of Indonesia, 1800–2000* (Honolulu: Allen & Unwin and University of Hawai'i Press, 2002), pp. 18–19.

31. W.S. Collinson, "Nautical Notices", *Asiatic Journal and Monthly Miscellany* 16 (1823): 258. This detail can be seen on the *Chart of Singapore Strait the Neighbouring Island and Part of Malay Peninsula* by J.B. Tassin, 1837.

32. Gretchen Liu, *Singapore: A Pictorial History, 1819–2000* (Singapore: Archipelago Press in association with the National Heritage Board, 1999), p. 102.

33. George Bogaars, "The Effect of the Opening of the Suez Canal on the Trade and Development of Singapore", *JMBRAS* 28, no. 1 (1955): 106; Mary Turnbull, *A History of Modern Singapore, 1819–2005* (Singapore: NUS Press, 2009), p. 104.

34. Carl Trocki, *Singapore: Wealth, Power and the Culture of Control* (New York: Routledge, 2006), p. 27.

5

A Seventeenth-Century Port Settlement in the Kallang Estuary

Kwa Chong Guan

Former Raffles Professor of History Wong Lin Ken commented that none of his colleagues has been able to explain the absence of any port on Singapore before Raffles arrived to establish one.[1] The implicit assumption underlying Wong's comment is that there should have been a settlement or port on Singapore because of its strategic location on the sailing and trading routes connecting the South China Sea and the Bay of Bengal. This essay attempts to connect the fragmentary evidence not available to the late Prof Wong and his colleagues to reconstruct a port settlement in the Kallang Estuary from the late sixteenth through much of the seventeenth century.

D'Erédia's 1604 Map

One of the maps drawn by the Portuguese-Malayan explorer (or *descobridor*, as he is described in contemporary accounts), cartographer and mathematician Manoel Godinho de Erédia in his *Declaram de Malaca e India Meridional com o Cathay* (Description of Melaka, Meridional India and Cathay) about his travels in the region at the beginning of the seventeenth century is of the Straits of Singapore.

It is unlikely de Eredia visited Singapore, but his map was based on information available to him.

The map, entitled "Chorographic description of the Straits of Sincapura and Sabban, 1604 A.D.", is oriented with Johor at the bottom of the map and Sumatra at the top. The map identifies several features on the east coast of "Sincapura". The northernmost feature identified is Tanjong Rusa, south of which are Tanah Merah, Sungei Bedok, Tanjong Rhu and a "Xabandaria", respectively. Tanjong Rusa refers to Changi Point today and may take its name from the shoals off its coast that were once known as Bĕting Kusah or Tanion Rusa, as Erédia marked it in his map. Tanah Merah refers to the red-orange weathered lateritic cliffs along the coast (which have been levelled today). They were a prominent landmark for navigators and pilots up to the nineteenth century.

It is similarly marked as "Red cliffs" in James Horsburg's 1806 chart of "Singapore and Malacca". Later sea charts distinguish between the "Red Cliffs" of Tanah Merah and Bedok. Other early maps of Singapore transcribed this old Malay place name as "Badok"—in the vicinity of the "small red cliff". Tanjong Rhu takes its name from the Malay *ru* or *ĕru* or *aru* for the casuarina trees (*C. equisetifolia* Linn) that grew on its sandy shores. The area was known as "Sandy Point" to the early nineteenth-century British settlers.

The significance of Eredia's map is its location of a "xabandaria" in the vicinity of Tanjong Rhu. The former puisne judge of the Straits Settlements Mr J.V. Mills, who was both a scholar and a colonial official, translated and edited a part of de Erédia's report in 1930. He failed, however, to note or comment on the reference to "xabandaria" in his study on de Erédia's report.[2] The last British director of the old Raffles Museum, the polymath Dr C.A. Gibson-Hill, verified de Eredia's four place names on the east coast of "Sincapura" in his detailed but underappreciated study of the charts and maps of the waters around Singapore. But he also did not comment on the reference to or significance of this "xabandaria".[3]

A "xabandaria" is also located on a circa 1654 map of the Singapore and Melaka Straits and the Riau archipelago by the Portuguese cartographer André Pereira dos Reis.

"Xabandaria"

"Xabandaria" is the Portuguese transcription of the Persian "Shahbandar"—literally, the "Lord of the Haven". In today's more prosaic language, the Shahbandar is a harbour master. The maritime laws of Melaka (*Undang-undang Melaka*) states in its opening paragraph that,

> Every king, must, in the first place, appoint a Chief Minister (Bendahara), second, a Police-Chief (Temenggong), third, a Treasurer (Penghulu

Bendahari) and fourthly, a Harbour-master (Shahbandar), so both the ruler and his subjects can live in peace and security.[4]

The Melaka sultans were continuing a centuries-old institution in appointing a shahbandar to administer trade in their harbour. It is an institution that not only the Melaka sultans but also most other rulers of port cities in island Southeast Asia and the Indian Ocean inherited from the Persian traders trading in the Indian Ocean and Southeast Asia to China from the middle of the first millennium of the current era into the eighteenth century, a period when Persian was the formal language of trade and governance.[5] The Dutch archives are filled with records of their East India Company traders having to negotiate with these shahbandars for permission to trade at ports along the coast of Kalimantan, the north coast of Java and in the eastern Indonesian islands.

Our best account comes from the Flemish gem trader Jacques de Coutre, who recorded in his *Memoirs* that he anchored before the "Shabandaria" of Singapore on his travels around the region in 1594. In his memorial to King Philip II of Spain, de Coutre recommended that his majesty consider building forts on Singapore or on the "Isla de la Sabandaria Vieja" (the Island of the Old Shabandaria) and "become the lord of this port, which is one of the best that serves the Indies".[6] Similarly, in the journals of the Dutch East India Company, Admiral Cornelis Matelieff de Jonge refers to a meeting in early May 1606 with the Shahbandar of Singapore, a Seri Raja Negara, who claimed to represent the Sultan of Johor residing upstream of the Johor River at Batu Sawar.[7]

Was this Shabandaria more likely to have been in the Singapore River or the Kallang estuary? The two maps and textual descriptions we have are imprecise on this issue. Recovery of some fragmentary archaeological evidence in the early 1970s suggests that this thriving "haven" was more likely to be in the estuary of the Kallang River.

In a British Admiralty file, ADM344, a 7 February 1819 "Sketch of the Land round Singapore" by hydrographers accompanying Sir Stamford Raffles on his expedition to establish an East India Company settlement at the southern end of the Strait of Melaka was found archived away. This sketch was found by historian Marcus Langdon while he was researching Penang's history in 2008, when the file was finally transferred to the National Archives, Kew, by the Admiralty.[8]

This sketch is important not only for being the earliest depiction of Singapore's waterfront, but it is also significant in that, besides the "Village of Singapore" in the Singapore River where Raffles met the Temenggong, there is also marked a "Ryat Village" around the entrance to the Kallang estuary. "Ryat", or *ra'yat* as transcribed today, would refer to an aboriginal village; in this instance, a village of sea nomads, possibly the Orang Biduanda Kallang, from whom the estuary takes its name.

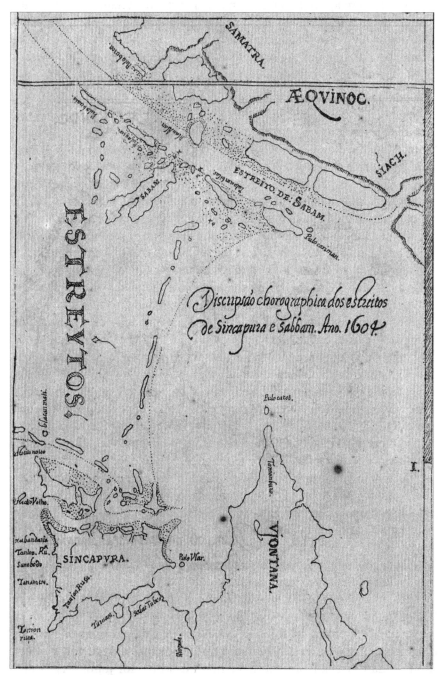

Figure 5.1 Map of Erédia, 1604. (Collection of National Library, Singapore. Accession no.: B03013605G)

This reference to a "Ryat Village" indicates another centre of activity besides the Singapore River, and may explain why Tengku Husein, after his recognition as sultan by Raffles, built his *istana* (palace) at Kampong Glam near to the Kallang Estuary, which was also the home of the Orang Biduanda Kallang and the seat of the Shahbandar and Seri Raja Negara in the seventeenth century.

Blue-and-White Porcelain from the Kallang Estuary

Another fortuitous event occurred during the dredging of the Kallang estuary in the late 1960s. The construction of the Benjamin Shears Bridge brought up, entirely by chance, evidence for seventeenth-century trading in the estuary. The dredge operator, Britisher Geoffrey Ovens, was sufficiently sharp-eyed to notice unusual objects being dredged up from the riverbed. Noticing this, he stopped the dredge and retrieved a sack of blue-and-white porcelain sherds from the mud. Sensing its inherent historical value, he called the old National Museum to ascertain the significance of what he had dredged up. As Ovens recounted to his friends in Singapore, including the author of this essay, the curators he spoke to expressed a marked disinterest in verifying his finds.

Those sherds were later distributed among friends of Ovens or discarded. Nine sherds were kept by a friend of Ovens, Ms Lee Geok Boi, who was persuaded by the present writer to loan them to the Oral History Department and National Archives for an exhibition in early 1986 on "Singapore Before Raffles". This exhibition was about the deep social memories of the Malay community, captured in interviews conducted by the Oral History Department. These nine sherds were subsequently displayed in the exhibition as supporting evidence for what the interviewees were recollecting from their deep social memories of life in the Kallang Estuary. Lee has since donated these sherds to the National Museum of Singapore, where they are now exhibited in its gallery on Singapore history. Geoffrey Ovens took with him on leaving Singapore a fairly intact pear-shaped vase and a large dish he had dredged up, which he prized. He willed that on his death these two artefacts be donated to the National Museum. And this is where they can be seen displayed prominently today.

The motifs on these nine sherds can be fairly precisely dated to the era of the Ming emperor Wanli (1573–1620).[9]

Michael Flecker, in his second essay in this volume, points out that some of the porcelain he recovered from the seventeenth-century Binh Thuan Wreck from South Vietnam destined for Johor has similar motifs to the sherds dredged up from the Kallang Estuary. The porcelain fragments we have were parts of wares that cracked or broke during the journey from China and were thrown overboard while the vessel they

Figures 5.2 and 5.3
Pear-shaped vase and
large dish. (Collection
of the National Museum
of Singapore, National
Heritage Board. Gift of
Geoffrey Ovens.)

Figure 5.4
The motif on the nine
sherds. (Collection of
the National Museum
of Singapore, National
Heritage Board. Gift of
Ms Lee Geok Boi.)

came in was anchored in the Kallang Estuary to take on fresh water
and other supplies. These eleven artefacts are now our only evidence
that there was trade being conducted in the Kallang estuary in the
seventeenth century. The recovery of these Wanli export ware sherds
suggests that the seventeenth-century Shahbandar's Office was more
likely to be in the vicinity of the Kallang Estuary than at the mouth of
the Singapore River.

Trading Networks of the Shabandaria of Singapore

Sherds like the eleven recovered from the Kallang Estuary have been
found in large quantities around Johor Lama and other sites occupied
by the descendants of the Melaka sultans who moved up the Johor River
to establish a new sultanate. The Heritage Conservation Centre of the
National Heritage Board (NHB) has in its collections several trays and
boxes of underglaze blue porcelain sherds and earthenware fragments
collected by staff of the old Raffles Museum during their field surveys

of Johor Lama and Kota Tinggi between 1948 and 1954.[10] Some of these sherds have been dated to the late fifteenth century, suggesting the existence of a riverine economy on the Johor River. This lively trade network would have attracted the descendants of the Melaka sultans to establish their new base there.

Marine archaeology excavations off the Vietnamese coast and the east coast of Malaysia from the late 1990s onwards have recovered a series of shipwrecks with large cargoes of Chinese and some Vietnamese or Thai porcelains. Michael Flecker, who excavated the wreck of a Chinese junk in 2002, states that it dates to 1608 and sank forty nautical miles east of the fishing port of Phan Thiet in Binh Thuan province, Vietnam. It was destined for Johor with a cargo of "silks and other Chinese goods". Flecker recovered approximately 60,000 pieces of Zhangzhou porcelains from the wreck.

The routes that the junk wrecked off Binh Thuan province and other vessels tracked from the south Chinese ports to their Southeast Asia destinations are recorded in rutters such as the *Shun feng xiang song* (Favourable winds in escort) and on a remarkable Chinese map found in 2008 in Oxford University's Bodleian Library. The map was acquired by the English jurist and "orientalist" John Selden, who willed it to the Bodleian Library in 1659.[11] This map, measuring 150 by 96 centimetres, is centred on the south China Sea and drawn according to early modern European cartographic standards. However, it also uses techniques of Chinese landscape painting to outline mountain ranges, rivers and ocean waves, giving the map the quality of a landscape painting. The key feature and significance of the map are the sixty ports it locates and connects by sailing routes that fan out from the major Chinese port of Quanzhou, with one principal route going northeast toward Nagasaki and another going southwest towards the Vietnamese port of Hoi An and on to the Malay peninsula.

What is significant about that southwards route is that Johor is depicted as its node, where the route then further branches out into sub-routes up the Melaka Strait, southwards along the Sumatran coast to the Sunda Strait, and westwards along the north Java coast. Another sub-route leads northeast towards Kalimantan and on to Manila, while yet another reaches out to the eastern Indonesian islands. Historians are still in the early stages of making sense of the map as a depiction of the Fujian or Hokkien maritime trading world in the late Ming period.

Conclusion

The fragmentary cartographic, textual and archaeological evidence colligated in this essay suggests that Singapore in the sixteenth century was re-emerging from the shadow of Melaka, which it was a fiefdom of in the fifteenth century, to become a regional trading centre. As in the fourteenth century—when Singapore served as a collection centre for local products from both its peninsula hinterland and its island foreland for export to other regional markets—so too in the sixteenth and seventeenth centuries, Singapore was again a regional entrepôt and entry point for traders sailing up the Johor River. The Dutch had a factory at Batu Sawar as they found it a good location to load pepper and distribute their Indian textiles. The gem trader De Coutre found Batu Sawar a centre of the diamond trade in the region. The Johor sultans appointed a Shahbandar on "the long island", or Pulau Panjang, as the island we know as Singapore was then better known, to administer trade entering the riverine economy they sought to control from their *istana* at Batu Sawar,[12] some forty-five kilometres upstream from the mouth of the Johor River. The Shabandaria on Singapore would have been the gateway to Batu Sawar.

Notes

1. Wong Lin Ken, "A View of Our Past", in *Singapore in Pictures*, edited by Lee Yik and Chang Chin Chiang (Singapore: Sin Chew Jit Poh and Ministry of Culture, 1981), p. 15.

2. J.V. Mills, "Eredia's Description of Malaca, Meridional India, and Cathay. Translated from the Portuguese with Notes", *Journal of the Malayan Branch of the Royal Asiatic Society* (*JMBRAS*) 8, no. 1 (1929): 1–288s.

3. C.A. Gibson-Hill, "Singapore Old Straits and New Harbour, 1300–1870", in *Studying Singapore before 1800*, edited by Kwa Chong Guan and Peter Borschberg (Singapore: NUS Press, 2018), pp. 221–308.

4. Liaw Yock Fang, *Undang-Undang Melaka: The Laws of Melaka* (The Hague: Nijhoff, 1976), p. 64. The *Undang-Undang Melaka* elaborates that "the Harbour-master is given jurisdiction over all matters concerning foreign merchants, orphans and all who have suffered injustice and furthermore, the regulations pertaining to junks, cargo-boats and other vessels".

5. On the extensiveness of this institution of the Shahbandar through the archipelago into early modern times, see Purnadi Purbatjaraka, "Shahbandars in the Archipelago", in *Studying Singapore before 1800*, edited by Kwa and Borschberg, pp. 354–65.

6. De Coutre's memorial, *Vida de Jaques de Coutre*, has been translated by Roopanjali Roy and edited by Peter Borschberg as *The Memoirs and Memorials of Jacques de Coutre: Security, Trade and Society in 16th- and 17th-Century Southeast Asia* (Singapore: NUS Press, 2014), p. 79, and memorial to King Philip II, p. 234.

7. Peter Borschberg, ed., *Journal, Memorials and Letters of Cornelis Matelieff de Jonge, Security, Diplomacy and Commerce in 17th Century Southeast Asia* (Singapore: NUS Press, 2015), p. 150. The shahbandar whom Matelieff

met was, however, more than a harbour master supervising trade. He was the Seri Raja Negara, a warrior or *hulubalang besar* of the sultan, who commanded the sea nomads or *orang laut* who formed the naval force of the sultan.

8. Marcus Langdon and Kwa Chong Guan, "Notes on 'Sketch of the Land Round Singapore Harbour, 7 Feb 1819'", *JMBRAS* 83, no. 1 (2010): 1–7.

9. The nine sherds are analysed in Kwa Chong Guan, "16th Century Underglazed Blue Porcelain Sherds from the Kallang Estuary", in *Early Singapore, 1300s–1819: Evidence in Maps, Texts and Artefacts,* edited by John Miksic and Cheryl-Ann Low Mei Gek (Singapore: Singapore History Museum, 2004), pp. 86–94.

10. G. de G. Sieveking, Paul Wheatley, and C.A. Gibson-Hill, "Recent Archaeological Discoveries in Malaya (1952–53). The Investigations at Johore Lama", *JMBRAS* 27, no. 1 (1954): 224–33. Also, C.A. Gibson-Hill, "Johore Lama and Other Ancient Sites on the Johore River", *JMBRAS* 28, no. 2 (1955): 127–97. Asyaari Muhamad and a team of senior archaeologists, including Nik Hassan Shuhaimi Nik Abdul Rahman and Kamaruddin Ab. Razak, undertook another series of archaeological excavations at Sayong Pinang, Panchor and Johor Lama between 1998 and 2010. Asyaari summarizes their findings in *Seramik Empayer Johor: Abad 11–19 masihi* (Kuala Lumpur: Jabatan Muzium Malaysia, 2012) and concludes from their analysis of the ceramic sherds collected that the Sungei Johor was a centre of trade before the sixteenth century.

11. The significance of the "Selden Map" in London's emergence as a global city in the seventeenth century is reconstructed in Robert K. Batchelor, *London: The Selden Map and the Making of a Global City, 1549–1689* (Chicago: University of Chicago Press, 2014). The relevance of the Selden Map for our understanding of the maritime history of the South China Sea is discussed in the papers in *New Research into the Maritime Trades, Seafaring and Underwater Archaeology of the Ming Dynasty: Hong Kong Maritime Museum International Symposium Proceedings*, edited by Tianlong Jiao et al. (Hong Kong: Hong Kong Maritime Museum and Chung Hwa Book Co, 2014). An accompanying exhibition catalogue *Mapping Ming China's Maritime World: The Selden Map and Other Treasures from the University of Oxford*, edited by Tianlong Jiao et al. (Hong Kong: Hong Kong Maritime Museum, 2015) includes a facsimile reproduction of the Selden map, a manual of compass directions, the *Shun feng xiang song* and another rutter, the *Zhi nan zheng fa* (The true art of pointing south).

12. Peter Borschberg, "Batu Sawar Johor: A Regional Centre of Trade in the Early Seventeenth Century", in *Early Modern Southeast Asia, 1350–1800*, edited by Ooi Keat Gin and Hoang Anh Tuan (Abingdon: Routledge, 2015), pp. 136–53. See also Peter Borschberg, "Urban Impermanence on the Southern Malay Peninsula: The Case of Batu Sawar Johor (1587–c.1615)", *Journal of East-Asian Urban History* 3, no. 1 (2021): 57–82.

6

The *Shah Muncher*

Michael Flecker

While excavating the fourteenth-century Temasek Wreck off Pedra Branca,[1] tidal overfalls were frequently observed, waves broke on submerged rocks, and intense squalls struck out of nowhere. All this during neap tides in the calm season. The wrecking potential of the rock outcrop at the eastern entrance of the Singapore Strait was very apparent.

In 1596, the Dutch merchant Jan Huygen van Linschoten wrote:

> From the Cape of Singapura to the hooke named Sinosura to the east, are 18 miles, 6 or 7 miles from thence lyeth a cliffe in ye sea called Pedra bianque, or White Rock, where the shippes that come and goe from China doe oftentymes passe in great danger and some are left upon it...[2]

Not just some. In Charles Buckley's 1902 work, *An Anecdotal History of Singapore*, he states:

> Between 1824 and 1851, sixteen large vessels were totally lost there [on Pedra Branca] and two others were stranded, besides other minor accidents.[3]

Figure 6.1 An 1882 painting of Pedra Branca before Horsburgh Lighthouse was built, with a European ship sailing by at a safe distance. (Painted by Captain Thomas Robertson [1819–73], based on an 1850 sketch by John Turnbull Thomson. Public domain, via Wikimedia Commons.)

Cursory examination of eighteenth-century records and nineteenth-century newspapers revealed the names of several of the ships "lost on Pedra Branca".

With a list of possible shipwrecks, and the potential discovery of more pre-European sites such as the Temasek Wreck, which were not recorded in state or company archives, the National Heritage Board (NHB) commissioned the Archaeology Unit (AU) of the ISEAS – Yusof Ishak Institute to carry out a search in the immediate vicinity of Pedra Branca. The rocky seabed precluded side-scan or multibeam sonar, so a magnetometer was deployed to detect cannons, anchors, iron cargoes or any other ferrous objects that could be associated with shipwrecks.

The search was conducted in mid-2019. After several fruitless dives on magnetometer hits, it was frustrating to discover that geomagnetic rock outcrops were causing the anomalies. But one anomaly was so big that it could only have been caused by a large quantity of iron. This turned out to be the twisted steel hull and cargo of the *MV Yu Seung Ho*, which had struck rocks and sank some three hundred metres east of Horsburgh Lighthouse in 1979. The magnetic anomaly was so pronounced and so extensive that it would have drowned out the subtle signatures of smaller iron objects in this most promising area. So it was back to basics with a diver visual survey.

Despite the poor visibility, tiny ceramic sherds were found within the steel wreckage. At first these pieces were thought to be broken crockery from the *Yu Seung Ho*'s galley. But after cleaning off the coral, it became evident that this was late eighteenth- or early nineteenth-century Chinese porcelain. A more extensive search resulted in the discovery of intact dishes and storage jars, and many broken bottles. During the last few days of the survey, two admiralty-pattern anchors were discovered, each 5 metres long. Together with fragments of copper hull sheathing and bronze spikes, the evidence increasingly pointed to a large European ship with a cargo of Chinese porcelain.

In 2020, a full-scale archaeological excavation commenced. Work began in a sediment-filled basin where surface finds suggested a high artefact concentration. Excavating from grid to grid towards the rocky shallows, many ceramic sherds and bottle fragments were recovered. So too were many polished agate medallions and hundreds of colourful glass beads.

While excavation progressed, the survey of the surrounding seabed continued. A bronze mortar was found on a rocky slope. At the top of the slope the seabed was found to be relatively flat between protruding boulders. Among those boulders lay a dozen or so cannons, all well camouflaged under a thick layer of iron concretion and coral. Eventually, twenty-four cannons were found, several of which had been completely buried. Another admiralty anchor, about 4 metres long, lay in the midst

Figure 6.2 Thousands of glass beads of many colours were found throughout the wreck site. (ISEAS)

Figure 6.3 Four heavily encrusted iron cannons lie on the seabed, one on top of the other at bottom right. (ISEAS)

Figure 6.4 A 5-metre long Admiralty Pattern anchor recovered from the wreck site. (ISEAS)

of the cannons. A little further to the east, near the shallowest rocks, a fourth anchor was discovered. At 5 metres, it was the same length as the two anchors that had been found during the initial survey, over 100 metres to the south-southwest. The shank and arms were thicker though, so this was probably the best bower anchor, which is the largest carried on board. The smaller one was a kedge anchor. The area was dubbed Cannon Flats. It was clearly the final resting place of the ship, in only 7 metres of water.

Remarkably, intact ceramics started to appear under layers of zinc ingots and ballast stones. Many of the bowls were decorated in blue-and-white, but the initial finds tended to be coarse ware. Finer porcelain finds were produced in the famed kilns of Jingdezhen, including underglaze blue-and-white, overglaze enamels and a combination of the two. Slightly lower grade wares came from Dehua. Many shapes were clearly made for the European market, including chafing dishes (warming plates), octagonal serving dishes, guglets (washing water bottles), mugs and teapots. Less common pieces included deep-blue monochrome jars, cups and bowls, dragon-decorated stoneware jars, earthenware herb boiling pots, crucibles and *yiqing* teapots. One *yiqing* teapot base was inscribed with the name of the famous Ming potter "Da Bin,

Figure 6.5 Divers sort newly recovered sherds surrounded by an array of intact and nearly intact dishes. Decorated with fu-dogs, dragons and horses, these dishes were made in the kilns of Dehua. (ISEAS)

a common late Qing forgery.[4] There was also a fascinating array of figurines, such as dogs, ducks, parrots, laughing Buddhas and *makara*. The *makara*, a mythical sea-creature, bears a striking resemblance to Singapore's Merlion.

Ship's fittings such as wooden pulley blocks, sheaves and a deadeye survived. So too did coils of rope of varying diameter, although the rope tended to disintegrate the moment it was exposed. In one sediment-filled pocket, a dozen or so bundles of string—called small stuff by old seafarers—were recovered. Far more robust were bronze piston buckets from the ship's bilge pumps. A total of eight were found, some with hinged valves still in place. At the base of the rocky slope, worm-eaten timbers were encased in torn copper sheathing. Eventually, several metres of linear timber were exposed, with a broken gudgeon marking the termination. Gudgeons formed the shipboard element of the giant rudder hinges. Hence these timbers were from the aft-most end of the keel, a structure called the deadwood. It must have broken away from the hull and collapsed downslope.

The only other coherent section of hull structure occurred adjacent to the kedge anchor. Five hull planks, up to 14 centimetres thick, were step-scarfed longitudinally. This construction technique provides a substantially stronger and more watertight structure than conventional carvel planking. While only fragments of frames remained in place, rows of fastening holes delineated their original positions.

Figure 6.6 A multi-hued *makara* figurine on the deck of the dive support vessel. (ISEAS)

Figure 6.7
A copper-alloy
piston bucket from
the *Shah Muncher*'s
bilge pumps, one
of eight recovered.
(ISEAS)

The array of non-ceramic artefacts was remarkable. Most obvious were literally hundreds of tonnes of highly corroded zinc ingots scattered throughout Cannon Flats. Apart from thousands of glass beads and agate medallions, there were intact cognac and wine bottles, silver-plated pots, mother-of-pearl stamps with Armenian script, a gold earring, fragments of carved ivory, bone hand-fan blades and brass clockwork mechanisms. Slabs and rolls of brass leaf emulated gold leaf. Copper alloy betel nut cutters and heavy chain bracelets rang of the Indian market. Amazingly, two types of percussion instrument survived: coconut shakers with wooden handles and wooden tambourines with brass jingles. Even fragile umbrellas survived, though not their waxed paper canopies.

Fourteen week-long expeditions were required to complete the excavation. With the wealth of material recovered, it was not so hard to identify the wreck. Focussed research eliminated most of those on the survey list. It turns out that "lost on Pedra Branca" also meant lost on nearby Middle Rocks or South Ledge, or even the fringing reef off northeast Bintan.

Only one documented late eighteenth- or early nineteenth-century ship was voyaging from China when she struck Pedra Branca. She is the *Shah Muncher*, a country ship that loaded in Canton and wrecked

Figure 6.8 A coconut shaker with a turned wooden handle. Red paint can still be discerned. (Flecker)

Figure 6.9 Excavating the figurine of a regal Chinese couple holding fans. Such a fine object may have been intended as a curio for a European buyer, although an overseas Chinese buyer is perhaps more likely. (ISEAS)

on 8 January 1796 while returning to her home port of Bombay. At 1,000 tons cargo capacity, she was similar in size to the larger East Indiamen trading between China and England. Country ships were privately owned European-designed and Indian-built merchant vessels that operated under licence from the East India Company. In order to maintain the Company's monopoly, they were only permitted to trade east of the Cape of Good Hope.

The *Shah Muncher* participated exclusively in the China–India trade. Every year from 1790 until the end of her short career, she voyaged from Bombay to Canton with a primary cargo of cotton. A surviving manifest provides a broad view of her last home-bound cargo: 585 tonnes of soft sugar; 483 tonnes of *tutenague* (zinc); 79 tonnes of sugar candy; 20 tonnes of porcelain; 15 tonnes of camphor; 2.5 tonnes of green tea; 2.3 tonnes of cotton cloth; 1.7 tonnes of umbrellas; and smaller quantities of black tea, cassia, raw silk, china root and tortoise shell. The total manifested cargo weight was 1,190 tonnes.

Relevant Contemporary Shipwrecks

There are several shipwrecks with similar cargo elements that went down shortly after the *Shah Muncher*. They occur throughout the world's oceans, placing the *Shah Muncher* in a very wide context of international maritime trade.

Sydney Cove

The *Sydney Cove* was lost on 9 February 1797, thirteen months after the *Shah Muncher*.[5] She was bound for Port Jackson (Sydney) having departed from Calcutta on 10 November 1796. The 250-ton vessel carried a speculative cargo that included 7,000 gallons of alcohol in bottles and casks, textiles, leather shoes, rice, sugar, tobacco, salted meat, livestock, and Chinese goods such as tea and ceramics. Storms in Bass Strait sprung her hull planking. In a sinking state, she was deliberately run aground off Preservation Island, one of the Furneaux Group, just north of Tasmania, Australia. As much as sixty per cent of the cargo was salvaged by the crew before the ship was smashed to pieces during a storm.

Archaeological excavations during the 1990s resulted in the recovery of 250 kilogrammes of Chinese porcelain, consisting of 160 kilogrammes of blue-and-white and 90 kilogrammes of polychrome overglaze ware of the so-called *famille rose* style. As this porcelain had probably been shipped from China to India in early 1796, it is not surprising that there are some close parallels with ceramics recovered from the *Shah Muncher*.

While the painted designs differ to some extent, some European types occur on both wrecks—namely, chafing dishes and guglets. Similar guglets were also recovered from the *Geldermalsen*, which sank in 1752.[6]

Valentine

On 16 November 1779, the British East Indiaman *Valentine* struck rocks off the small island of Brecquou in the Guernsey Islands, at the entrance to the English Channel. Sailing from Bombay and Madras for London, she carried four thousand bags of saltpetre, several hundred bales of raw silk and "18 boatloads of red dyewood", along with private trade goods.[7]

Archaeological recoveries during the 1970s included sherds of Chinese blue-and-white porcelain and worked agate. The truncated square and rectangular pieces of agate are identical to those from the *Shah Muncher*. Green speculates that the agate on the *Valentine* was cut and shaped in India for the English market, where it would have been set in signet rings and broaches.[8] There are several surviving examples of Georgian jewellery featuring mounted agate of this shape. The *Shah Muncher*'s outward manifest demonstrates that agate was also in demand in China. But demand was insufficient to absorb the 100,000 pieces supplied on the outward voyage from India. The thousands of pieces found on the wreck were returning surplus.

Diana

Like the *Shah Muncher*, the *Diana* was a country ship, but she traded from Calcutta rather than Bombay.[9] At a tonnage of 350, she was much

Figure 6.10 Excavating a blue-and-white porcelain chafing dish from the *Shah Muncher*. Similar chafing dishes were recovered from the *Sydney Cove*. (Flecker)

Figure 6.11 A selection of cut and polished agate medallions recovered from the *Shah Muncher*, which are identical to those found on the *Valentine*. (Courtesy of the Asian Civilisations Museum, Singapore)

smaller than the 1,000-ton *Shah Muncher*, conforming to the norm for relative ship sizes at these two Indian ports. On 5 March 1817, around midnight, the *Diana* became stranded on a rock just north of Melaka while voyaging from Canton to her home port. She slipped off and sank in deeper water at dawn the following morning. Her surviving manifest lists alum, green tea, nankeens (cotton cloth), silk pieces, camphor, sugar candy, cassia, china root, white lead, soft sugar, 18 tons of chinaware and 2 tons of glass beads. Most of these categories of cargo items had also been loaded aboard the *Shah Muncher* for her various return voyages from China.

The repertoire of ceramic shapes on the *Diana* was relatively limited. There were large quantities of so-called "starburst" and "om" plates.[10] On the *Shah Muncher*, there are a few "starburst" sherds and a few more "om" sherds, demonstrating that these designs were long-lived. *Diana* also carried many finer quality blue-and-white ceramics, collectively forming elaborate European dinner services. Several were decorated with the "Fitzhugh" pattern made up of four decorative medallions around a central circular element, while others adopted the popular "willow" pattern. Elongated octagonal serving dishes and chafing dishes are replicated on the *Shah Muncher*, but with a more sophisticated version of the "willow" pattern. Both wrecks also carried European wine bottles, which would seem to have been for shipboard use.

Figure 6.12 Four octagonal serving dishes recovered from the *Shah Muncher*. They are more elaborately decorated than similar dishes on the *Diana*. (ISEAS)

Tek Sing

The *Tek Sing* struck a rock and sank in the Gasper Strait, Indonesia, in 1822 while en route from Canton to Batavia. She was a Chinese junk of immense proportions, perhaps even larger than the *Shah Muncher*. Tragically, there were as many as 2,000 people on board, some 1,600 of them coolies destined for the sugar plantations of Java. Fortuitously, passing by at the time, Captain Pearl managed to rescue 190 people, taking them aboard his ship, *Indiana*. The rest perished. The wreck was discovered in 1999 and salvaged a year or so later. A staggering 350,000 ceramic items were recovered.[11]

In common with the *Shah Muncher*, which sank twenty-six years earlier, are petal-*lingzhi* pattern dishes and bowls, Dehua bowls with a band of circles around the rim, *yiqing* teapots with characters inscribed on the base, and European wine bottles.

Desaru Wreck

The Desaru *Wreck*, lying off the town of that name on the east coast of peninsular Malaysia, is a Chinese junk that is thought to have sunk between 1821 and 1830.[12] Her ceramics cargo parallels that of the *Diana* and the *Tek Sing*, with "om" and "starburst" dishes and *yiqing* teapots being common. Of the total 63,000 intact ceramics recovered, some 50,000 were Chinese spoons. There were Chinese spoons of varying types on the *Shah Muncher*.

Tuara Wreck

The Tuara Wreck has been dated to the late eighteenth century from her ceramics cargo, although it could perhaps be the early nineteenth century given the extended use of many decorative motifs.[13] Several of the types are similar to the *Shah Muncher* ceramics, although the European shapes are absent. She is a Chinese junk that wrecked on a reef to the northwest of Makassar, Sulawesi, Indonesia.

Other Shipwrecks Framing Pre-colonial Singapore

The *Shah Muncher* wrecked twenty-three years before Raffles re-established the port of Singapore. The *Diana* passed through the Singapore Strait just two years before, briefly stopping at Melaka before wrecking a day out. The Desaru ship may well have been bound for Singapore, with a lifetime supply of Chinese spoons. But what of earlier shipping? What can older shipwrecks tell us of Singapore's context before the arrival of Raffles?

Ca Mau Wreck

The Ca Mau Wreck was found and partly looted by fishermen in 1998 before the Vietnamese government stepped in to conduct an excavation.[14] Reign marks on the recovered porcelain point to a date range of 1723 to 1735. Blue-and-white porcelain made up the majority of the surviving cargo, with bowls, dishes, vases, jars, cups and ewers. A wide range of enamelled decorative items, such as "dragon houseboats" and zoomorphic figurines, attest to an interest in curios. There were some fine celadon pieces and some underglaze reds and blues added to the mix. This was no doubt a cargo of Chinese ceramics for the European market, destined for trans-shipment at Batavia.

Most shipments from China to Batavia at this time were made by Chinese junks. But from the very limited archaeological evidence, this may not be the case with the Ca Mau ship. A timber from the wreck has been identified as *Dipterocarpus* genus, which only occurs in Southeast Asia. A plank said to be from the wreck had two wooden dowels protruding from an edge-joint. The Chinese did not use wooden dowels. It is extremely unfortunate that the hull was not fully recorded in-situ, for this may have been the first archaeological evidence of a Southeast Asian *jong*, the successor to the lashed-lug design that was phased out in the early fourteenth century.

Vung Tau Wreck

The Vung Tau Wreck was excavated in the south of Vietnam in 1991.[15] She turned out to be a *lorcha*, a ship combining the best of Chinese and Portuguese shipbuilding traditions, and the only one ever documented so far. She carried a diverse cargo, ranging from floor tiles to iron cauldrons to paint pigment. But the main surviving cargo type was porcelain. Stylistic analysis of the porcelain dates the wreck to the Kangxi period (1662–1722). A cyclic date inscribed on an ink stick narrows it down further to 1690 or shortly thereafter.

Blue-and-white porcelain from the Jingdezhen kilns included vases, jars, dishes, teacups and saucers, teapots, covered boxes, wine cups, flutes, chalices, mugs, kendis and candle holders. Beautiful examples of whiteware from Dehua included cups, saucers, spoons, covered boxes, jarlets, and figurines of dogs, crabs and the goddess Guanyin. Provincial ware made up a large proportion of the ceramics cargo, mostly in the form of blue-and-white and overglaze enamel bowls.

The European shapes of much of the Jingdezhen blue-and-white, and depictions of Dutch canal houses on some large vases, strongly suggest that this cargo was bound for trans-shipment onto a European vessel. Much of the whiteware would have followed. But, without exception, all the other trade goods loaded on the Vung Tau ship were Chinese in origin and Chinese in use, and all point to the resupply of a Chinese enclave. As with the Ca Mau Wreck, Batavia is the obvious candidate.

Wanli Wreck

The Wanli Wreck[16] brings to light a higher quality Chinese export ware. The cargo was mostly Jingdezhen blue-and-white *kraak* porcelain. The wreck was named after early finds suggested the Wanli period (1573–1619). But subsequent in-depth analysis puts the date closer to 1625. A study of the hull remains and the condition of the cargo suggest she was a relatively small Portuguese-flagged ship, perhaps built in India, and that she exploded. This may have been during a battle with the Dutch while returning to Melaka from Macao.

Her cargo comprised an estimated 37,000 pieces of porcelain, although the explosion caused extensive breakage. Magnificent dishes, bowls, ewers, covered boxes, and bottles were probably intended to be trans-shipped for the onward voyage to Europe.

It is interesting to note that this extensively researched ship could not be identified in the Portuguese archives. This may be partly explained by the loss of much archival material in the Lisbon earthquake and subsequent fire of 1755. But it is possible that few records were kept of locally built ships in the intra-Asia trade. We may be ignorant of a significant trade network.

Binh Thuan Wreck

The Binh Thuan Wreck was excavated off southern Vietnam in 2002.[17] She was found to be a Chinese junk loaded with cast iron pans and Zhangzhou porcelain. While archival material concerning individual junk losses does not appear to exist in China, there is occasional mention in European archives.

On 21 July 1608, Abraham van den Broecke, the Johor representative of the newly formed Dutch East India Company (VOC), penned a report to his superiors at the Dutch factory in Banten, Java, stating:

> We have received the news that I Sin Ho, the Chinese merchant, while returning with his junk [to Johor] was lost at sea somewhere about Cambodia. For that reason the VOC loses 10 piculs of raw silk and other Chinese goods.

In the seventeenth century, Dutch charts refer to Cambodia, a large part of eastern Thailand and southern Vietnam simply as "Cambodia". Having a ceramics cargo consistent with a Wanli date, and lying off ancient Cambodia, there is a high probability that the Binh Thuan ship belonged to I Sin Ho. If so, she was destined for Johor.

Manoel Godinho d'Erédia's 1604 chart of the "Straits of Sincapura and Sabbam" clearly depicts a "Shabandaria", or harbour master's location, on the southern coast of Singapore. Likewise, this is marked on the 1654 chart of André Pereira dos Reis. If I Sin Ho was bound for Johor, he would most likely have called at the Shabandaria in Singapore first. Interestingly, some porcelain from the Binh Thuan Wreck bears the same decorative motif as Wanli (1573–1620) sherds that were dredged from the Kallang River in the late 1970s, although the latter were a product of Jingdezhen.

Discussion

Trade linked major ports in China with those in Europe, often via a host of secondary ports in South and Southeast Asia. Behind these trade networks was an array of participants: European, Chinese, Indian and Southeast Asian. A wide variety of goods were carried in all directions. From China came ceramics, iron, silk, sugar and tea. From India came cotton and opium. From Southeast Asia came tin and a multitude of jungle and sea products. Europe supplied woollens to China, and silver dollars to everyone, but other European products were not so popular. Consequently, the Europeans participated in secondary trade to gain a foothold in Southeast Asian markets. Chinese porcelain was a key commodity in that secondary trade.

European ships built in Europe and in India, Chinese junks, Southeast Asian *jongs* and hybrid *lorchas* plied Asian seas. The China–

Figure 6.13 A painting of the *Surat Castle*, a sister ship of the *Shah Muncher*. The larger merchant ships first calling at Singapore would have appeared just like her. (Public domain, via Wikimedia Commons)

Java trade, exemplified by the Ca Mau and Vung Tau wrecks, bypassed the Singapore Strait. However, well before the arrival of Raffles, Singapore served as a base for Johor's Shabandaria, and was therefore the likely destination of the Binh Thuan ship. There is a chance that the Wanli ship, a small Portuguese trader, called at Singapore as a secondary port on the heavily utilised trade route between the South China Sea and the Indian Ocean, Melaka being the primary port.

The *Shah Muncher* passed close by Pulau Satumu, the site of Raffles Lighthouse, eleven times on her voyages between Bombay and Canton. She sometimes stopped off at the British settlement on Prince of Wales Island, now Penang. But she never did drop anchor in Singapore's harbour; nor did the country ship *Diana*. However, the more recent *Desaru* junk, hugging the Malaysian coast on her way south from China, may indeed have been destined for the newly established British outpost of Singapore.

Along with the Tuara Wreck and the *Tek Sing*, the Desaru Wreck demonstrates that late eighteenth- to early nineteenth-century Chinese blue-and-white porcelain, of varying quality, was exported in Chinese junks as well as in European ships, with final destinations ranging from India to England and from Java to eastern Indonesia. It is a ubiquitous product that also shows up in excavations, in collections and as heirlooms in Singapore.

Who Was Onboard the *Shah Muncher*?

A wonderful photograph dated 1855–62 shows the action on the quarterdeck of a country ship weighing anchor. The scene would have been much the same six decades earlier. We may conjecture as follows: Captain Anson Smith stands cockily at the quarterdeck rail. His mate stands barefoot on the companion way, overseeing the lascars manning the windlass. Following tradition, a fiddler encourages the crew to bend to their labours. A senior lascar takes the helm, while others climb the ratlines or stand by to hoist sail. Behind the mate stands a moustachioed European merchant, with his elaborately dressed and no doubt uncomfortable wife. And behind her, from his headdress, we may well have a cleric of the Armenian Apostolic Church.

It is interesting that Parsi built and owned ships were usually under the command of British captains. Perhaps this is because the ships were of European design, with their inherent multitude of sails and rigging. Trade in Canton was conducted in collaboration with the East India Company, so British captains would also be well placed to deal with their countrymen. Occasionally, county ships were called into battle alongside British warships and merchantmen against European rivals—

notably the French. It would have been a great advantage to have likeminded commanders.

Lascars were Indian ship's crew, while sepoys were Indian soldiers serving the British. Sepoys were not deployed on country ships, but the line between the two blurred, as lascars also manned the cannons to fend off pirates and rivals.

With a large part of the "Chinaware" and tea cargo destined for trans-shipment to Britain, it comes as no surprise that European merchants travelled on country ships. The many bottles found on the *Shah Muncher* once contained beer, wine, rum, brandy and cognac for the consumption of the ship's officers and accompanying merchants. Three mother-of-pearl stamps, a tiny gold tag and an ornate silver rosewater sprinkler all display Armenian script, a clear sign that Armenian merchants and perhaps clerics were also onboard. Chinese locks may well have been on unaccompanied chests, but a Chinese scale-weight, a coin and remnants of an inkstone are likely to have been the possessions of attendant Chinese merchants.

Apart from marvelling at the cosmopolitan nature of the likely crew and passengers onboard the *Shah Muncher*, we may also envisage the

Figure 6.14 The quarterdeck of a country ship. (Image made available courtesy of DeGolyer Library, Southern Methodist University. Public domain, via Flickr Commons.)

first non–East India Company visitors to Singapore in 1819. Of course, Chinese junks and Southeast Asian ships were attracted to the duty-free port, where many of their passengers would have settled. But the country ships had been passing through the Singapore Strait twice a year for well over half a century. Cargoes shipped between India and China would have been similar to those traded at Singapore, so there was good reason for country ships to drop anchor mid-voyage. They may well have brought the first Indian residents, Parsis in particular, and the first Armenians.

Conclusions

The *Shah Muncher* was a country ship launched in India in 1789. Country ships were privately owned merchant vessels that operated under license from the East India Company. But to maintain the Company's monopoly, they were only permitted to trade between Indian Ocean ports, Australian settlements and within Asia.

On 8 January 1796, the heavily laden *Shah Muncher* was forced upon the rocks of Pedra Branca by the current. Much of the accessible cargo was probably salvaged by local seafarers, although the ongoing monsoon would have hindered this task for some months.

Over the process of fourteen week-long excavations, including two for the recovery of large artefacts such as cannons and anchors, the full extent of the wreck site was revealed. Work started in the Basin to the northwest and proceeded up the rocky slope before focusing on the densely packed shallows. A remarkable degree of stratigraphy revealed the wrecking process, whereby heavy destructive elements such as ballast stones and zinc ingots have astonishingly protected the underlying ceramics. Porcelain that survived intact until burial was ensured longevity.

The range of recovered ceramics is extensive in both type and decoration. They were made in the kilns of Jingdezhen, Dehua and various provincial potting centres. Stoneware storage jars were probably made in Guangdong, but they were not an export item in themselves. They contained liquids and organic materials for trade and for shipboard use.

The *Shah Muncher* is the largest of the very few country ships that have been excavated. As far as can be ascertained, she is the only one that was bound from China to India when lost. The surviving manifest provides a broad view of her cargo, consisting, in order of tonnage: soft sugar, zinc, sugar candy, porcelain, camphor, green tea, cotton cloth, umbrellas, black tea, cassia, raw silk, china root and tortoise shell. The total recorded cargo weight was 1,190 tonnes.

The archaeological finds paint a much more vivid picture. Some non-ceramic artefacts were for shipboard use, such as bronze mortars and bottles of wine. But most were for trade and not included on the manifest. They include stone plinths, agate medallions, glass beads, betel nut cutters, bracelets, silver-plated pots, and brass leaf. Surviving ship's gear includes anchors, cannons, bilge pump valves, deadeyes, pulley blocks, sheaves and rope. Isolated coherent hull structure suggests great strength via thick hull planking with full-length longitudinal scarfs.

The *Shah Muncher* sank twenty-three years before Raffles re-established the port of Singapore. With many country ships remaining in service for decades, had she not come to grief on the rocks of Pedra Branca, the *Shah Muncher* may well have been one of the first ships to drop anchor in Singapore, the midway point on her regular round trip from Bombay to Canton. Her sister ships may have brought the first Parsi and Armenian settlers. Her cargo would not have changed much, thereby providing an idea of the types of goods purchased by Singapore's fledgling community, along with those that would have been trans-shipped. The fleets of East India Company ships that first traded at Singapore would have looked just like the *Shah Muncher*. However, if they were homeward bound, they would have carried more tea than sugar.

Whether visited, or simply admired while sailing by, Singapore was central to the complex Asian maritime trade network throughout the pre-colonial period. An analysis of shipwrecks spanning several centuries suggests that some were likely to have been destined for Singapore. With the establishment of a duty-free port in 1819, Singapore waters would have played host to a wide array of ships: European ships built in Europe and in India, Chinese junks, Southeast Asian *jongs* and hybrid *lorchas*.

The *Shah Muncher*, despite never dropping anchor off Singapore, remains of great relevance to Singapore's maritime past.

Notes

1. Michael Flecker, *The Temasek Wreck (mid-14th Century), Singapore – Preliminary Report*, Temasek Working Paper Series no. 4 (Singapore: ISEAS – Yusof Ishak Institute, 2022).

2. Jan Huygen van Linschoten, *The Voyage of John Huyghen van Linschoten to the East Indies. From the Old English Translation of 1598* (London: Hakluyt Society, 1855), p. 119.

3. Charles Buckley, *An Anecdotal History of Singapore: (With Portraits and Illustrations) From the Foundation of the Settlements under the Honourable the East India Company, on February 6th, 1819, to the Transfer to the Colonial Office as Part of the Colonial Possessions of the Crown on April 1st, 1867*, vol. 2 (Singapore: Fraser & Neave, 1902), p. 510.

4. Tai Yew Seng, personal communication.

5. Mark Staniforth and Michael Nash, *Chinese Export Porcelain from the Wreck of the Sydney Cove (1797)*, Australian Institute for Maritime Archaeology Special Publication no. 12 (Adelaide: Brolga Press for the Australian Institute for Maritime Archaeology, 1998).

6. Colin Sheaf and Richard S. Kilburn, *The Hatcher Porcelain Cargoes: The Complete Record* (Oxford: Phaidon, 1988), p. 140.

7. Valentine Excavation Group, *Valentine: First Years Work on the British East Indiaman* (n.p. 1976).

8. Georgina Green, "Valentines, the Raymonds and Company Material Culture, in *The East India Company at Home, 1757–1857*, edited by Margot Finn and Kate Smith (London: UCL Press, 2018), pp. 231–50.

9. Dorian Ball, *The Diana Adventure* (Kuala Lumpur: Malaysian Historical Salvors, 1995).

10. Rows of dense, stylized Sanskrit characters for the sacred "om" syllable extend around the circumference of these plates.

11. Nigel Pickford and Michael Hatcher, *The Legacy of the Tek Sing: China's Titanic – Its Legacy and its Treasures* (London: Granta Editions, 2002).

12. Sten Sjøstrand, Adi bin Haji Taha, and Samsol Sahar, *Mysteries of Malaysian Shipwrecks* (Kuala Lumpur: Department of Museums, 2006), p. 100.

13. Michael Flecker, "Three 18th-century Shipwrecks off Ujung Pandang, Southwest Sulawesi, Indonesia: A Coincidence?", *International Journal of Nautical Archaeology* 28, no. 1 (1999): 45–59.

14. Nguyen Dinh Chien, *Tàu Cổ' Cà Mau: The Ca Mau Shipwreck 1724–1735* (Hanoi: National Museum of Vietnamese History, 2002).

15. Christiaan J.A. Jörg and Michael Flecker, *Porcelain from the Vung Tau Wreck: The Hallstrom Excavation* (UK: Sun Tree, 2001).

16. Sten Sjøstrand and Sharipah Lok Lok binte Syed Idrus, *The Wanli Shipwreck and its Ceramic Cargo* (Kuala Lumpur: Department of Museums, 2007).

17. Michael Flecker, "The Binh Thuan Wreck (Containing the Complete Archaeological Report)", in *Christie's Australia: The Binh Thuan Shipwreck* (Melbourne: Christie's, 2004).

7

Singapore and the Country Trade in the Late Eighteenth and Early Nineteenth Centuries

Peter Borschberg

The *Shah Muncher* was a British country trader that was on its return voyage in 1796 from China to Bombay when it sank off the rocky outcropping of Pedra Branca. The British port of Singapore had of course not then been founded, but it is well within the realm of possibility that the ship travelling westward intended to call at one of the nearby ports of the Singapore and Melaka Straits. This might have been Riau (approximately today's Tanjung Pinang) on the island of Bintan, or perhaps even Melaka, where the ship could have taken on fresh water and provisions before sailing on to India.

This chapter does not discuss the ship or its cargo as such, but rather outlines in broad strokes the economic and political context in which the *Shah Muncher* was operating. To this end, the temporal scope of this chapter straddles the eighteenth and the early nineteenth centuries. It is perhaps opportune to define at this juncture the nature of the seaborne trade we are concerned with. What is country trade? And what is a country trader? Simply put, country trade refers to private trade within (or sometimes outside of) an established trading monopoly. European country trade in the Indian Ocean reaches back to the time of the earliest Portuguese explorers and adventurers at the turn of the 1400s and 1500s. But the most familiar monopoly would be the one held by the British East India Company based in London towards the modern period. Even though country trade could and did assume different forms, the term generally refers to private trade in certain commodities between specific ports. Linked to the country trade, the expression "country trader" then refers either to a natural person who carried out the trade, usually the captain or owner of the vessel who sailed under a particular national flag—in the specific case of the *Shah Muncher* it would refer to the British flag—or could otherwise refer to the entire ship. It should be stressed that private or country traders hailing from different parts of Europe became active in seaborne trade, especially in the Western Pacific and Indian Ocean during the second half of the eighteenth and early nineteenth centuries.[1]

Why did chartered companies grant trading licences to private traders? First, enforcing the chartered monopoly of the company could prove to be very costly as it involved deploying maritime assets to enforce compliance, suppress smuggling and identify interlopers. In addition, most of the European chartered companies were unable to effectively suppress private trade among their employees. There are many tales of poorly paid mariners whose sea chests, when opened after their owner's death at sea, contained many high-value compact trading goods that could never have been purchased with their modest salaries.[2] Add to this the difficulty of throwing off a profit on all trading goods on all shipping routes. In order to conserve capital, companies decided to farm out the trade along less profitable routes and in commodities that did not yield a high margin. By the end of the eighteenth century, chartered companies came to focus increasingly on such routes in commodities that could generate significant profits. Many European countries permitted such private trade explicitly—or at least closed an eye to it—with the Dutch representing something of an exception during the period of the United Netherlands East India company, or VOC (Verenigde Oostindische Compagnie), up until around the year 1795.[3] The Dutch had always been wary of compromising the company's monopoly by opening up trade to private persons, even if such trade already existed on an informal basis.

In the case of British trade, country trade was formally permitted after 1796. From this point onwards, country trade opened up progressively, such as with Java in 1811 and private trade with India in 1813. The British East India Company retained its profitable position in the tea trade until the last vestiges of its trading monopoly with China ceased in 1833. All of these changes attracted new country traders to the Indian Ocean and Western Pacific regions. As a rule, country traders procured a pass or licence to trade from one of their colonial ports or from an outpost of one of the East India companies. Several of these European companies were active in India. In addition to the British, they included the Danes and the French. Country traders sometimes sailed on their own account, but they might also lease their ship with crew to one of the chartered companies. This appears to have been the case with the *Shah Muncher*. Leasing ships with crew had distinct advantages. It allowed the chartered companies to respond quickly to shifts in trading demand and capacity and prevented them from being saddled with a rapidly depreciating asset or groups of employees who regularly needed to be paid their salaries.

Given the proximity of the country traders to the East India companies, it is worth offering a few thoughts on how these early modern chartered companies operated in broad terms. The companies operated on the basis of mercantilist economic thinking, which in Britain reached its apex in the second half of the seventeenth century, though some mercantilist policies survived well into the eighteenth and even nineteenth centuries.[4] Mercantilists measured national wealth in terms of how much bullion or coinage circulated in the national economy. For this reason, the export of gold and silver in minted or un-minted form was heavily restricted. Chartered companies like the VOC soon understood that they had to generate income in their charter region first, which they used to finance imports into Europe. These imports consisted in the early phase of colonial trade chiefly of spices and other exotica from Asia, and from the seventeenth century onwards increasingly also textiles and stimulants (tea and coffee). Famously, London's East India Company financed its purchases of tea in China with opium that the company procured in South and Western Asia. Traders in this type of commerce also bartered goods procured in India, China or the Malay Archipelago around the ports of the Indian Ocean and Western Pacific rim. Towards the close of the eighteenth century, country traders had formed synergies with each other and also separately with institutions such as agency houses. These agency houses were responsible for granting credit or determining the different types of trading goods that were needed. They helped to establish and maintain trading circuits between India, Southeast Asia and China. What emerges was a circular trade: textiles and cottons from India were exchanged in Southeast Asia for spices, marine and jungle produce. Other items used for barter and trade included stimulants like opium and weapons.

Country traders (understood here as natural persons) fulfilled functions that extended well beyond the functions of a simple trader. They were often proficient in one of the local languages—such as Malay—a skill that helped them to understand local customs and values. Through their long involvement in these circuits, these country traders gradually built up direct contacts with local rulers or their trading proxies, and in some instances acted as personal envoys by conveying letters and missives of a diplomatic nature.[5] Over many years, the country traders acquired a solid grasp of the trading risks associated with a port or polity, especially in the region of the Malay Peninsula. Such familiarity with the unique trading risks aided knowledge formation. Collecting and systematizing data about coasts, waters, trading routes or even the presence of pirates made an important contribution towards charting and mapping, especially of the Singapore and Melaka Straits region. Country traders came to know where supplies and food provisions could be readily procured, and also in what quantities.[6]

Against this backdrop, it is evident that country traders played a significant role in opening up British commerce with and expanding knowledge of the Malay states in the late eighteenth and early nineteenth centuries. They were especially active, however, in the decades between 1780 and 1820, a period when country traders were engaged in tasks on behalf of the British East India Company, and their activities in the Straits and around the Peninsula resulted in greater British interest in the region.[7] This took place against the backdrop of burgeoning private trade between India and China, especially after 1813. The liberalization of trade broadly coincided with the global commercial boom that followed the end of the French Revolutionary and Napoleonic Wars.

As seaborne commerce between India and China grew towards the end of the 1700s, the British increasingly felt that they required a base or foothold in the Singapore and Melaka Straits region. Ships heading through the Straits in the direction of India or China often called at Melaka in order to take on provisions and fresh water. But, by 1795, Melaka was a loss-making outpost under the rule of the Dutch East India Company. By the final quarter of the eighteenth century, three main locations were considered for a British post, starting with the Malay-Bugis port of Riau on the island of Bintan. In late 1784, the Dutch defeated the forces of the Bugis and the Malays, and by law of war and conquest took possession of the historic Johor-Riau Sultanate, which also included Singapore.[8] The British, under the country trader Thomas Forrest, were keen to gain a permanent foothold in the region and sought to negotiate the acquisition of Riau from the Dutch, but to no avail.[9]

Shortly after the Dutch defeat of Johor-Riau, Francis Light acquired the island of Penang for Britain and subsequently founded a factory and settlement, Georgetown. It was soon discovered, however, that Penang was not ideally located and it was deemed to be too far removed from the main shipping artery through the Singapore and Melaka Straits.[10] In 1795, Melaka came under British trusteeship during the period of the French Revolutionary and Napoleonic Wars, and remained under British administration for a period of a little over three decades.[11] During this time, Melaka acted—albeit temporarily—as a British base in the region. The port and some surrounding lands were returned in 1818 to the newly formed kingdom of the Netherlands, in line with the 1814 London Convention.[12]

While the British country traders were expressing their dismay at the transfer of Malacca back to Dutch suzerainty, the Dutch were having a different set of discussions: Melaka under the VOC had been a loss-making outpost, and it was expected that a Melaka returned to Dutch rule in the early nineteenth century would be no different. Plans were touted in the early 1800s by the Dutch to focus their attention on a different part of the Malay Peninsula and Western Malay Archipelago, which included a potential site at or near Singapore.[13] By the final weeks of 1818, the issue of the British post and provisioning station in the Singapore and Melaka Straits region was being seriously discussed again. Additional locations contemplated by the British authorities in India included Simangka Bay on Sumatra near the Sunda Strait, Banjarmasin on the island of Borneo, the island of Belitung located off the coast of central-eastern Sumatra, and the port of Riau. Many of these initiatives were scuppered by higher authorities in Calcutta and London.[14] Following the end of the Napoleonic Wars and the carving out of the new kingdom of the Netherlands from the former first French Empire, the British wanted to give the Dutch the opportunity to consolidate their power and position in Europe and were wary of antagonizing their neighbours in the Malay Archipelago. The island of Karimun, the Johor River estuary in general and the island of Singapore were all identified as potential locations for the new British factory and outpost, but they all fell under the rule of the Johor-Riau Sultanate. Justifying their actions by interfering in the succession dispute and interpreting the structure of the Johor-Riau Sultanate as a loose confederation independent from the political centre,[15] Major William Farquhar and Thomas Stamford Raffles recognized Johor's contender to the throne as the new sultan and signed a treaty with him and with the Temenggong (as the legal "owner" of Singapore and adjacent isles). This agreement permitted the establishment of a British factory and post on Singapore. It is important to bear in mind that this initial treaty, signed in 1819, only granted the British the right to set up a British factory (or factories) on the island. It was not accompanied by any extensive land grant that would have permitted planning and construction of a substantial settlement under British rule. Activity in the port and markets was to be jointly administered by the British, Sultan Husain and the Temenggong Abdul Rahman. This "condominium of Company officials and Malay rajas", as the historian Christopher Wake dubbed the situation, soon proved problematic.[16] By 1824, the British moved to acquire full sovereignty over Singapore and the adjacent islands within a radius of ten geographical miles.[17]

The founding of British Singapore did antagonize the Dutch, who initially contemplated military action to remove the British from the island. Convinced of the legal merits of the case, however, the Dutch refrained from this, but they insisted that the new British factory on Singapore represented a violation of international treaties and infringed upon the sovereignty of the Johor-Riau sultan Abdul Rahman. Debate surrounding the legal merits of British Singapore eventually gave way to deliberations on its utility and expediency to the Empire sometime between 1819 and 1823. This shift was partially the outcome of the British traders and their proxies in Britain's Parliament as they steered public debate and shifted public opinion in Britain.[18]

In fact, British traders played an important role in propelling Singapore's early success. What shape this took has been documented and studied in detail by the former Raffles Professor of History at the University of Singapore Wong Lin Ken.[19] Together with the agency houses, British traders played an important role as pioneers of commerce on the island. Among the important agency houses forming synergies with the country traders were A.L. Johnston, founded in 1819; Harrington & Co. and John Purvis, both founded in 1820; T.O. Crane, founded in 1825; and Guthrie & Co., founded in 1833.[20]

Concluding Thoughts

To sum up, the *Shah Muncher* was a country trader that was sailing from China when it sank near the rocky outcropping of Pedra Branca in 1796. This took place in a period when the East India company showed a growing interest in the Straits region and in gaining a foothold for the burgeoning trade along the India to China route. British Singapore had not yet been established, but the *Shah Muncher* would certainly have passed the island upon which Singapore's British settlement would be founded, and it may have intended to call at Riau or Melaka to take on water and provisions. While the *Shah Muncher* missed the founding of Singapore by a little more than two decades, the ship was clearly following a maritime route that was well frequented by other European country traders of this era. In cooperation with the agency houses, these British country traders gave Singapore a significant boost to its early commerce and early cargo throughput, as has been discussed in many earlier publications.

Notes

1. For an overview of secondary studies touching on European (including British) country trade in the Indian Ocean, Western Pacific and Strait of Melaka, see Martin Krieger, "Konkurrenz und Kooperation in Ostindien: Der europäische country-trade auf dem Indischen Ozean zwischen 16. und 18. Jahrhundert", *Vierteljahresschrift für Sozial- und Wirtschaftsgeschichte* 84, no. 3 (1997): 322–55; D.K. Bassett, "British 'Country' Trade and Local Trade Networks in the Thai and Malay States, 1680–1770", *Modern Asian Studies* 23, no. 4 (1989): 625–43; Dianne Lewis, "The Growth of the Country Trade to the Straits of Malacca, 1760–1777", *Journal of the Malaysian Branch of the Royal Asiatic Society (JMBRAS)* 43, no. 2 (1970): 114–30.

2. For an example, see Peter Borschberg, ed., *Journal, Memorials and Letters of Cornelis Matelieff de Jonge. Security, Diplomacy and Commerce in 17th-Century Southeast Asia* (Singapore: NUS Press, 2015), p. 329.

3. For the situation in the VOC during the final decades of its corporate lifespan, see Chris Nierstrasz, *In the Shadow of the Company: The Dutch East India Company and Its Servants in the Period of Its Decline (1740–1796)* (Leiden: Brill, 2012).

4. For an overview, see the useful article by Alain Clement, "English and French Mercantilist Thought and the Matter of Colonies during the 17th Century", *Scandinavian Economic History Review* 54, no. 3 (2006): 291–323.

5. See, especially, W.G. Miller, "English Country Traders and Their Relations with Malay Rulers in the Late Eighteenth Century", *JMBRAS* 84, no. 1 (2011): 23–45.

6. The Singapore and Melaka Straits region suffered from a particularly poor reputation with respect to piracy. For an account covering this period, see Carl A. Trocki, *Prince of Pirates: The Temenggongs and the Development of Johor and Singapore, 1784–1885* (Singapore: NUS Press, 2007).

7. See the somewhat dated but still helpful account by K.C. Tregonning, *The British in Malaya: The First Forty Years 1786–1826* (Tucson: University of Arizona Press, 1962).

8. For this episode, see the account by Elisa Netscher, *De Nederlanders in Djohor en Siak, 1602 tot 1865* (Batavia: Bruining, 1870); also, Reinout Vos, *Gentle Janus, Merchant Prince: The VOC and the Tightrope of Diplomacy in the Malay World, 1740–1800* (Leiden: KITLV, 1993).

9. D.K. Bassett, "British Trade and Policy in Indonesia, 1760–1772", *Bijdragen tot de Taal-, Land- en Volkenkunde van Nederlandsch-Indië* 120, no. 3 (1964): 197–223; Nicholas Tarling, *The Anglo-Dutch Rivalry in the Malay World* (Brisbane: Cambridge University Press, 1962), p. 40; Kwa Chong Guan, Derek Heng, Peter Borschberg, and Tan Tai Yong, *Seven Hundred Years: A History of Singapore* (Singapore: Marshall Cavendish and National Library Board, 2019).

10. See Tregonning, *The British in Malaya*, 1962.

11. See Graham Irwin, "Governor Couperus and the Surrender of Malacca, 1795", *JMBRAS* 29, no. 3 (1956): 86–133; D.K. Bassett, "The Surrender of Dutch Malacca, 1795", *Bijdragen tot de Taal-, Land- en Volkenkunde* 117, no. 3 (1961): 344–58.

12. For additional background, see Pieter Hendrik van der Kemp, *De Teruggave der Oost-Indische Koloniën, 1814–1816* (The Hague: Nijhoff, 1910); P.H. van der Kemp, "De Stichting van Singapore, de Afstand ervan met Malakka door Nederland, en de Britische Aanspraaken op den Linga-Riouw-Archipel", *Bijdragen tot de Taal-, Land- en Volkenkunde van Nederlandsch-Indië* 10 (1902): 313–476; and Peter Borschberg, "Dutch Objections to British Singapore", *Journal of Southeast Asian Studies* 51, no. 1 (2019): 540–61.

13. Ibid.

14. Tregonning, *The British in Malaya*, 1962, p. 147.

15. This interpretation was advocated by Charles Assey as well as Raffles and the Marquess of Hastings. See, especially, Charles Assey, *On the Trade with China and the Indian Archipelago, with Observations on the Insecurity of the British Interests in that Quarter*, 2nd ed. (London: Printed for Rodwell and Martin, 1819), pp. 50–51.

16. C.H. Wake, "Raffles and the Rajas: The Founding of Singapore in Malayan and British Colonial History", *JMBRAS* 48, no. 1 (1975): 47–73, esp. p. 63. For additional background, see also Kwa Chong Guan, "Singapore in 1819: The Beginnings of a New Kerajaan", in *Studying Singapore before 1800*, edited by Kwa Chong Guan and Peter Borschberg (Singapore: NUS Press, 2018), 366–84.

17. Peter Borschberg, "The 1824 Treaties", in *200 Years of Singapore and the United Kingdom*, edited by Tommy Koh and Scott Whitman (Singapore: Straits Times Press, 2019), pp. 48–55.

18. Concerning the shift in British public opinion, see Dianne Lewis, "British Policy in the Straits of Malacca to 1819 and the Collapse of the Traditional Malay State Structure", in *Empires and Imperialism in Southeast Asia*, edited by Brook Barrington (Clayton, Victoria: Monash Asia Institute, 1997), pp. 17–33; Howard L. Malchow, *Gentlemen Capitalists: The Social and Political World of the Victorian Businessman* (Palo Alto: Stanford University Press, 1991), esp. pp. 83–109.

19. Wong Lin Ken, *The Trade of Singapore, 1819–69* (Kuala Lumpur: Malaysian Branch of the Royal Asiatic Society, 1961); earlier published as a long article in *JMBRAS* 33, no. 4 (1960): 4–315. Separately, also, L.K. Wong, "Singapore: Its Growth as an Entrepot Port, 1819–1941", *Journal of Southeast Asian Studies* 9, no. 1 (1978): 50–84.

20. For the role of the early agency houses in Singapore, see Peter J. Drake, *Merchants, Bankers and Governors: British Enterprise in Singapore and Malaya, 1786–1920* (Singapore: World Scientific, 2017).

Index

Page references in bold refer to figures. Numbers prefixed by "n" refer to notes.